MARY BERRY'S
TELEVISION COOKBOOK

Macdonald

Contents

Editorial Manager
Chester Fisher

Editor
Linda Sonntag

Design
Mushroom Production   London

Production
Penny Kitchenham

© Macdonald Educational Ltd 1979

Text © Thames Television Ltd 1979

Published in association with
Thames Television's programme
After Noon Plus produced by
Catherine Freeman

The material in this book first
appeared in *Family Cooking*
and *Family Recipes* both
published in 1978.

First published 1979
Macdonald Educational Ltd
Holywell House
Worship Street
London EC2A 2EN

ISBN 0 356 06797 1

Made and printed by
Purnell & Sons Ltd., Paulton

Introduction

This is the latest all-in-one *After Noon Plus* cook book. It combines my favourite family recipes from previous volumes in one bargain bumper edition.

If, like me, you have a husband and children with healthy appetites, then you will need to know how to satisfy them *and* get value for money. You will want to make sure they get all the goodness they need, without breaking the household budget.

With the help of this book you can make simple wholesome dishes that all the family will enjoy and for next to nothing. There is even a recipe for a hearty nourishing soup made from the trimmings of leeks and sprouts! Other sustaining meals include traditional fare like steak and kidney pudding and more exotic dishes from the Continent, which are rapidly becoming my own children's favourites like Moussaka and Lasagne.

Though I am always aware of the importance of spending wisely, I know that food is often the best treat of the day for adults as well as children. So I have included a selection of delicious ice-cream recipes, mouth-watering desserts and sumptuous cakes and puddings. This will cover your requirements for the whole year from light and refreshing fruit salads through cheesecakes to tried and tested staples like bread and butter pudding. At the other end of the scale there are more elaborate concoctions of chocolate and meringue.

There is a special section of Christmas recipes including Classic turkey roast and Christmas pudding and I have given extra thought to other special occasions like dinner parties, where you might want to spend a little more to make the meal one to remember, and picnics and outdoor brunches.

Most of these recipes have already been demonstrated on *After Noon Plus*, or will be featured in the future, and I hope that this double volume will satisfy the appetites of your family as it has mine, for some time to come.

Soups

Iced Spanish soup

2 × 14 oz cans tomatoes
1 large onion, peeled
1 large green pepper, seeds and
 pith removed
half a cucumber, peeled
3 small cloves garlic, peeled
2 tablespoons chopped parsley
2 slices white bread without
 the crusts
salt and freshly ground
 black pepper
3 tablespoons wine vinegar
3 tablespoons oil
a few drops of Tabasco sauce
½ pint iced water

2 × 380 gm cans tomatoes
1 large onion, peeled
1 large green pepper, seeds and
 pith removed
half a cucumber, peeled
3 small cloves garlic, peeled
2 tablespoons chopped parsley
2 slices white bread without
 the crusts

salt and freshly ground
 black pepper
45 ml wine vinegar
45 ml oil
a few drops of Tabasco sauce
300 ml iced water

A soup for a summer's day. Serve ice cold with side dishes of cubed cucumber, cubed red and green pepper, and diced onion. You could add fried croutons of bread too.

Place all the ingredients together and purée in an electric blender in two or three batches until smooth. Turn into a bowl and mix well. Chill in the refrigerator for 2 to 3 hours. Check seasoning. Serve the soup very cold with an ice cube in each bowl and the side dishes suggested above. Serves 6.

Fresh leek soup

2 oz butter
1½ lb leeks, cleaned and finely
 chopped
1 oz flour
1 pint home-made stock or
 2 chicken stock cubes
 dissolved in 1 pint water
salt and pepper
½ pint milk
a little single cream if liked

50 gm butter
675 gm leeks, cleaned and finely
 chopped
25 gm flour
600 ml home-made stock or
 2 chicken stock cubes
 dissolved in 600 ml water
salt and pepper
300 ml milk
a little single cream if liked

Melt the butter in a large saucepan. Add the leeks and fry gently stirring occasionally without browning for 5 minutes. Stir in the flour and cook for 2 minutes.

Gradually add the stock, stirring continually. Add seasoning and milk, bring to the boil and simmer for 40 minutes. Taste and check seasoning and if liked add a little cream. Serves 4.

Add single cream before serving for special occasions, about ¼ pint (150 ml) is plenty.

Remove the bayleaf then sieve or liquidize the soup in a blender. Taste and check seasoning and if the soup should be too thick, thin down with a little extra stock. Serves 4.

Frugal soup

8 oz sprouts and trimmings
1 leek
1 oz butter
¾ pint water
1 chicken stock cube
1 oz flour
½ pint milk
large pinch grated nutmeg
salt and pepper

225 gm sprouts and trimmings
1 leek
25 gm butter
450 ml water
1 chicken stock cube
25 gm flour
300 ml milk
large pinch grated nutmeg
salt and pepper

Cut down on waste by using the outside leaved of sprouts for this soup.

Wash and roughly chop the sprouts and trimmings, thoroughly wash the leek and cut in slices.

Melt the butter in a pan and add the leek, cover and cook gently for 5 minutes, add the water, stock cube and sprouts and bring to the boil. Simmer uncovered for 15 minutes or until tender, then sieve or puree in the blender.

Blend the flour with a little of the milk, then stir in the remainder. Return the soup to the pan and stir in the milk and flour. Bring to the boil, stirring until thickened, season with nutmeg and salt and pepper. If the soup should be a little too thick, thin down with stock or milk. Serves 4.

Good carrot soup

1 lb carrots
1 small onion
1 oz butter
1¼ pints chicken stock or
    1¼ pints water and 2 chicken
    stock cubes
3 strips of orange peel
1 bayleaf
salt and pepper

450 gm carrots
1 small onion
25 gm butter
750 ml chicken stock or
**   750 ml water and 2 chicken**
**   stock cubes**
3 strips of orange peel
1 bayleaf
salt and pepper

For special occasions add swirls of cream or yoghurt to the soup before serving.

Peel and slice the carrots and onions. Melt the butter in a pan and add the vegetables, cover and cook gently for 5 to 10 minutes. Pour on the stock or water and stock cubes and add the strips of orange peel (take the peel from the orange with a potato peeler). Add bayleaf and seasoning and bring to the boil. Cover and simmer for about 15 minutes or until the carrots are tender.

Lemons filled with sardine pâté

4 small lemons
2 oz butter, softened
2 oz cream cheese
4½ oz can sardines in oil
ground black pepper

4 small lemons
50 gm butter, softened
50 gm cream cheese
125 gm can sardines in oil
ground black pepper

Cut a thin slice from the base of each lemon so that they stand flat, then cut a larger slice from the top of each lemon and scoop out the insides using a grapefruit or serrated knife and strain through a sieve.

Cream the butter and cheese together. Drain the sardines, mash with a fork, and beat into the butter with 2 tablespoons (30 ml) of the strained lemon juice and plenty of black pepper.

Pile the mixture into the lemon shells, top each with a lid and serve on individual plates. Serves 4.

This makes an inexpensive starter and looks very pretty with each lemon garnished with a fresh bay leaf.

Smoked mackerel pâté

2 smoked mackerel
10 oz butter, melted but not hot
4 oz cream cheese
juice of ½ lemon
small sprigs of parsley

2 smoked mackerel
275 gm butter, melted but not hot
100 gm cream cheese
juice of half a lemon
small sprigs of parsley

Remove the skin and bones from the mackerel and put the fillets with 8 oz (225 gm) of the butter, the cream cheese and the lemon juice in the blender in two batches and blend until smooth.

Divide the pâté between 6 individual serving dishes and smooth the tops or put in a small loaf-shaped tureen or dish, about 1 pint

(600 ml) size. Spoon on a little of the remaining butter, remelted so that it pours on top of each dish and leave in a cool place until set.

Serve garnished with small sprigs of parsley and with hot toast and butter. Serves 6.

For a milder flavour make this pâté using smoked trout.

Potter's pâté

1 large onion
8 oz chicken livers
8 oz pork sausagemeat
1 heaped tablespoon chopped
  parsley
1 level teaspoon salt
pinch ground black pepper
2 cloves garlic, crushed
about 5 rashers streaky bacon

1 large onion
225 gm chicken livers
225 gm pork sausagemeat
1 heaped tablespoon chopped
  parsley
1 level teaspoon salt
pinch ground black pepper
2 cloves garlic, crushed
about 5 rashers streaky bacon

Peel and quarter the onion and pass through the mincer with the chicken livers or put in the blender and purée. Turn into a large bowl with the sausagemeat, parsley, seasoning and garlic, mix well together.

Remove the rind and bone from the bacon, place on a board and spread flat with the back of a knife. Line the bottom and sides of a 1 lb or 1½ pint (450 gm or 900 ml) loaf tin, with the bacon rashers, put in the meat mixture and spread flat.

Cover the tin with a piece of foil, place in a roasting tin half filled with hot water, and cook at 325°F, 170°C, Gas No. 3 for 1½ hours.

The pâté is cooked if, when the centre is pierced with a skewer, the juices that run out are clear and it has slightly shrunk from the edges of the tin.

Lightly weight the pâté with weights, or tins on top of a piece of wood covered with foil and leave to become quite cold. Serve sliced with hot toast and butter. Serves 6.

Surprisingly easy to make — a very good all-purpose pâté. Ideal for a first course, equally delicious for a picnic.

Kipper pâté

10 oz frozen kipper fillets, thawed
¼ pint double cream
pinch cayenne pepper
sprig parsley

300 gm frozen kipper fillets,
  thawed
150 ml double cream
pinch cayenne pepper
sprig parsley

Cook kipper fillets according to the directions on packet. When they are cooked, remove them from bag. Pour the butter into a mixing bowl and set aside.

Remove all dark skin and any bones from kipper fillets. Add kipper fillets to bowl with cream and cayenne. Mash ingredients together with a fork until smooth. Alternatively, mix all the ingredients together in an electric blender. Spoon pâté into a serving dish and smooth the top. Chill for at least 2 hours. Garnish with parsley and serve with hot toast and butter. Serves 4.

In the unlikely event that you have any leftovers of this delicious pâté you will find that children love it as a sandwich filling.

Melon and prawns in sour cream

1 small melon
a little shredded lettuce
4 oz frozen prawns, thawed
5 oz carton soured cream, chilled
1 rounded teaspoon chopped
  mint
small sprigs of mint

1 small melon
a little shredded lettuce
100 gm frozen prawns, thawed
150 ml carton soured cream,
  chilled
1 rounded teaspoon chopped
  mint
small sprigs of mint

I often do this easy first course when melons are reasonably priced. Serve a non-fruity dessert to follow. Take care to thaw the prawns slowly in the fridge and dab off every drop of liquid before blending with the cream.

Cut the melon in half and remove all the seeds. Scoop out the flesh into balls and leave to chill in the refrigerator.

Place a little shredded lettuce in the bottom of 6 glasses.

Thoroughly dry the prawns on kitchen paper and drain off any juice from the melon. Put in a bowl with the cream and chopped mint and blend lightly. Divide between the glasses, garnish each with a small sprig of mint and serve at once. Serves 6.

Country pâté

1 egg
¼ lb salt belly of pork
¾ lb green bacon pieces
¾ lb pig's liver
2 shallots or 1 onion
2 oz lard
1 oz flour
2 cloves garlic, crushed
plenty of ground black pepper
4 tablespoons sherry or port
1 level tablespoon freshly chopped
   mixed herbs
6 crushed juniper berries
To garnish: 2 bay leaves

1 egg
100 gm salt belly of pork
350 gm green bacon pieces
350 gm pig's liver
2 shallots or 1 onion
50 gm lard
25 gm flour
2 cloves garlic, crushed
plenty of ground black pepper
60 ml sherry or port
1 level tablespoon freshly
   chopped mixed herbs
6 crushed juniper berries
To garnish: 2 bay leaves

Check with the butcher if the belly of pork has been salted and if it has soak overnight before using.

Skin and bone the belly and roughly cut up. Remove the rind and bone from the bacon and trim

the liver. Peel and roughly chop the shallots and fry in the lard for 4 to 5 minutes.

Mince the pork, bacon, liver and shallots, add the remaining ingredients and mix well. Pour the mixture into a greased 2 pint (a good 1 litre) dish, lay the bay leaves on top, cover with a piece of foil and stand in a dish of hot water and cook at 325°F, 170°C, Gas No. 3 for 1½ to 2 hours.

Remove from the oven. The pâté is cooked if when the centre is pierced the juices that run out are clear and it has shrunk slightly from the edges of the dish.

Lightly weight the pâté with weights, tins or a piece of foil-covered wood and leave to become quite cold.

Serve sliced with French bread or hot toast. Serves 10.

It is always difficult to tell whether you have seasoned a pâté to your liking. This is what to do: when the pâté is made and ready to go into the dish, take a spoonful of the mixture and fry it gently in butter for 5 minutes or so, turning in the pan, then taste this sample and adjust seasoning by adding a bit more salt, pepper and herbs.

Curried egg mayonaise

6 hard-boiled eggs
6 tablespoons home-made
   mayonnaise
3 teaspoons lemon juice
2 tablespoons mango chutney
   juice
1 teaspoon curry powder
salt and pepper
sprigs of cress

6 hard-boiled eggs
6 tablespoons home-made
   mayonnaise
3 teaspoons lemon juice
2 tablespoons mango chutney
   juice
salt and pepper
sprigs of cress

If you boil the eggs for only 9 or 10 minutes and then cool them quickly under running water until absolutely cold, you will avoid an unsightly black ring around the edge of the yolk.

Cut the hard-boiled eggs in half lengthways and set out on a serving dish. Make the mayonnaise as on p. 22 and blend it with the lemon juice, chutney juice, curry powder and salt and pepper. Spoon the mixture over the eggs and decorate with sprigs of cress. Serves 6.

Pork galantine

4 thin slices ham
8 oz pork sausagemeat
1 lb finely minced lean pork
3 oz slice cooked ham, diced
3 oz slice cooked tongue, diced
1 heaped teaspoon salt
ground black pepper
1 level teaspoon chopped
 lemon thyme
grated rind of 1 lemon
1 egg
12 whole stuffed green olives

4 thin slices ham
225 gm pork sausagemeat
450 gm finely minced lean pork
75 gm slice cooked ham, diced
75 gm slice cooked tongue, diced
1 heaped teaspoon salt
1 level teaspoon chopped
 lemon thyme
grated rind of 1 lemon
1 egg
12 whole stuffed green olives

Heat the oven to 325°F, 160°C, Gas No. 3 and line an oval 1½ pint (1 litre) casserole or terrine with the slices of ham.

Thoroughly blend all the other ingredients together and spread in the dish, cover with a piece of foil and stand in a meat roasting tin half filled with hot water. Bake in the oven for 1½ to 2 hours depending on the depth of the dish

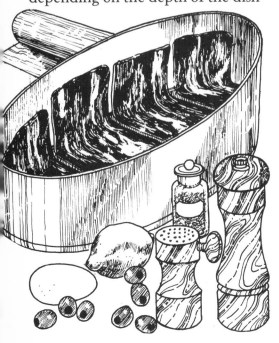

— a deep dish will take a little longer. The galantine is cooked when it has shrunk slightly from the sides of the dish and when a skewer inserted in the middle causes the juice to run clear.

Leave to become quite cold then chill overnight in the refrigerator. Turn out and serve sliced with salads. Serves 6.

A true galantine is first boiled in a pudding cloth in the shape of a sausage; this is a rather messy process and I prefer to make it using an oval casserole to get the shape.

Swedish salad platter

Eggs Indian style
Halve two hard-boiled eggs lengthwise and lay cut-side down along the edge of a large serving dish. Blend a little mayonnaise with a good pinch of curry powder, squeeze of lemon juice and a little mango chutney juice and spoon over the eggs. Sprinkle each egg with paprika pepper.

Cucumber and dill
Toss slices of peeled cucumber in a little French dressing that has had some chopped fresh dill tips added to it and spoon in a line onto the dish alongside the egg mayonnaise. Decorate with dill.

Ham rolls
Finely dice a large cooked potato and mix with 2 sticks sliced celery and a chopped eating apple. Add just sufficient mayonnaise to bind well together. Place a spoonful of the mixture on each of the 4 slices of ham and roll up. Place in a line on the dish alongside the cucumber and dill salad.

Tomato and onion
Peel and slice 8 oz (225 gm) tomatoes and mix with a very finely sliced onion. Lightly toss in a little French dressing and spoon onto the plate alongside the rolls. Sprinkle with a few finely chopped chives.

This is a colourful salad dish which may be served as an hors d'oeuvre. It also makes an attractive addition to any buffet meal. Serves 4.

Cheese aigrettes

1 oz butter
¼ pint water
2 oz self-raising flour
1 egg yolk
1 egg
2 oz mature Cheddar cheese,
    grated
salt
cayenne pepper

25 gm butter
150 ml water
50 gm self-raising flour
1 egg yolk
1 egg
50 gm mature Cheddar cheese,
    grated
salt
cayenne pepper

Put butter and water in a small saucepan and bring to the boil. Remove from the heat and add the flour, beat well until the mixture is glossy and leaves the sides of the pan clean, cool slightly.

Lightly mix the yolk and the egg together and beat into the mixture a little at a time. Stir in the cheese, salt and a pinch of cayenne pepper, check seasoning.

When required, drop the mixture in heaped teaspoonfuls into hot deep fat and fry gently until golden brown, turning once. Lift out and drain on kitchen paper. Serve at once. To freeze: open-freeze then pack in a container, label and return to freezer. To serve, defrost for about 2 hours at room temperature and the heat in a hot oven at 425°F, 220°C, Gas No. 7, for about 10 minutes. Makes about 16 cheese aigrettes.

Serve as a savoury course or as a snack with drinks.

Cheese soufflé

1½ oz butter
1½ oz flour
½ pint hot milk
salt and pepper
1 level teaspoon made mustard
4 oz strong Cheddar cheese,
    grated
4 large eggs

40 gm butter
40 gm flour
300 ml hot milk
salt and pepper
1 level teaspoon made mustard
100 gm strong Cheddar cheese,
    grated
4 large eggs

Heat the oven to 375°F, 190°C, Gas No. 5 and place a baking sheet in it. Melt the butter in a pan, stir in the flour and cook for 2 minutes without browning. Remove the pan from the heat and stir in the hot milk. Return to the heat and bring to the boil, stirring until thickened, then add the seasoning and mustard and leave to cool.

Stir in the cheese. If preferred use 3 oz (75 gm) strong Cheddar cheese and 1 oz (25 gm) grated Parmesan. Separate the eggs and beat the yolks one at a time into the cheese sauce. Whisk the egg whites with a rotary hand or electric whisk until stiff, but not dry. Stir one heaped tablespoonful into the cheese sauce and then carefully fold in the remainder.

Pour into a buttered 2 pint (a good litre) soufflé dish, run a teaspoon around the edge of the dish and bake on a hot baking sheet in the centre of the oven for about 40 minutes until well risen and golden brown. Serve at once. Serves 3 to 4.

Variations:
Choose any flavouring and add to the mixture before the egg yolks.

Ham: add 4 to 6 oz (100 to 175 gm) ham or boiled bacon, finely chopped.

Fish: add 4 to 6 oz (100 to 175 gm) finely flaked cooked smoked haddock.

Shellfish: add 4 oz (100 gm) peeled prawns or shrimps.

Mushroom: add 8 oz (225 gm) finely chopped mushrooms, cooked in 1 oz (25 gm) butter.

Spinach: add 1 lb (450 gm) cooked finely chopped spinach with a pinch of nutmeg and topped with a little grated cheese.

This makes a delicious light lunch, but if you prefer, serve it as a first course baked in small ramekins. In smaller dishes the soufflé will only take about 20 minutes to cook.

Fish for supper

Italian tuna bake

6 oz spaghetti
salt
2½ oz butter
2 oz flour
1 pint milk
freshly ground black pepper
½ level teaspoon mustard
4 oz Cheddar cheese, grated
1 large onion, sliced
7 oz can tuna fish, drained and
    roughly flaked
2 hard-boiled eggs, chopped

175 gm spaghetti
salt
65 gm butter
50 gm flour
600 ml milk
freshly ground black pepper
a little mustard
100 gm Cheddar cheese, grated
1 large onion, sliced
200 gm can tuna fish, drained
    and roughly flaked
2 hard-boiled eggs, chopped

Cook the spaghetti in boiling salted water until tender, about 10 minutes. Drain and rinse thoroughly.

Melt 2 oz (50 gm) butter in a saucepan, add flour and cook for 1 minute. Gradually add the milk and bring to the boil, stirring frequently. Add 1 level teaspoon salt, pepper to taste and mustard and simmer for 2 minutes. Remove from the heat and stir in 3 oz (75 gm) cheese until melted.

Fry the onion in the remaining butter until golden brown, then drain. Lightly grease a 3 pint (1.7 litre) ovenproof casserole and place half the spaghetti in the bottom, pour over half the sauce, cover with the tuna fish, onions and chopped

eggs. Finally lay the remaining spaghetti on top and pour the rest of the sauce over. Sprinkle with the remaining cheese.

Cook in the oven at 400°F, 200°C, Gas No. 6 when required for about 1 hour or until hot through and the top is well browned. Serves 4.

This is convenient to assemble the day before you bake. Makes a different family supper dish that needs no vegetables, just hot crisp French bread for the hungry ones. If your family is not fond of tuna you could use chopped ham or bacon joint instead.

Fish and egg pie

1 lb cod
1 pint milk
2 oz butter
2 oz flour
1 level teaspoon salt
¼ level teaspoon white pepper
2 level tablespoons chopped
    parsley
pinch nutmeg
4 hard-boiled eggs, quartered
1½ lb potatoes, peeled

450 gm cod
600 ml milk
50 gm butter
50 gm flour
1 level teaspoon salt
pinch white pepper
2 level tablespoons chopped
    parsley
pinch nutmeg
4 hard-boiled eggs, quartered
675 gm potatoes, peeled

Wash the fish, put in a saucepan with the milk and simmer gently for 10 minutes or until the fish can be flaked with a fork. Strain the milk from the fish, then skin the fish and flake, removing any bones.

Rinse out the pan, then melt the butter in it and stir in the flour. Cook for 2 minutes, then stir in the milk and cook the sauce for about 2 minutes, stirring until thickened. Add salt, pepper, nutmeg, parsley and the flaked fish, mix well. Taste and check the seasoning and lightly fold in the quartered eggs.

Turn into a shallow 3 pint (1½ litre) ovenproof dish and leave to cool. Boil the potatoes, drain, and mash with milk and butter; taste and season. Spread over the fish and mark the top with a fork.

Reheat when required in a hot oven 425°F, 220°C, Gas No. 7 for about 30 to 40 minutes. Serves 6.

A great stand-by for Saturday lunch for a crowd. I double up the recipe, make it the day before, or even a couple of weeks ahead, then freeze it. For a large pie I find it best to brown it under the grill first, then to reheat it at 325°F, 170°C, Gas No. 3, for about an hour until the dish is piping hot through.

minute, add the milk and bring to the boil, stirring until thickened.

Place the gelatine in a small bowl with the water and leave to soak for a few minutes, then add to the sauce and stir until dissolved. Put the white sauce and flaked fish in a blender and purée until smooth. Turn into a large bowl and leave to cool.

Add the mayonnaise and lemon juice to the sauce and fold in the whipped cream and hard-boiled eggs. Taste and check the seasoning and either turn into a 2 pint (1 litre) dish or into 6 to 8 individual ramekins.

Chill until firm and set, and garnish each ramekin or the large dish with small sprigs of parsley or watercress. Serves 6 to 8.

Fish and egg pie

Make either as one large mousse or in individual ramekin dishes. Serve with a tossed green salad and thin brown bread and butter.

Smoked haddock mousse

1 lb smoked haddock
½ pint milk
freshly ground black pepper
1 oz butter
¾ oz flour
½ oz powdered gelatine
   (1 packet)
2 tablespoons water
scant ½ pint homemade or good
   bought mayonnaise
juice of 1 lemon
¼ pint double cream, whipped
2 hard-boiled eggs,
   finely chopped
small sprigs parsley or watercress

450 gm smoked haddock
300 ml milk
freshly ground black pepper
25 gm butter
19 gm flour
12.5 gm powdered gelatine
   (1 packet)
30 ml water
scant 300 ml homemade or good
   bought mayonnaise
juice of 1 lemon
150 ml double cream, whipped
2 hard-boiled eggs,
   finely chopped
small sprigs parsley or watercress.

Place the fish in a shallow pan, pour over the milk and season with pepper. Poach gently for about 10 minutes or until the fish flakes easily. Drain the fish, reserving the milk, and flake, removing all the skin and bones.

Melt the butter in a small saucepan and stir in the flour, cook for a

Family meat dishes

Steak and kidney

1 lb skirt beef
4 oz ox kidney
1 rounded tablespoon flour
1 small onion, finely chopped
4 oz mushrooms, sliced
1 level teaspoon salt
¼ level teaspoon pepper
about ¼ pint stock

Suet Pastry:
8 oz self-raising flour
1 level teaspoon salt
3 oz shredded suet
8 tablespoons cold water

450 gm skirt beef
100 gm ox kidney
1 rounded tablespoon flour
1 small onion, finely chopped
100 gm mushrooms, sliced
1 level teaspoon salt
¼ level teaspoon pepper
about 150 ml stock

Suet pastry:
225 gm self-raising flour
1 level teaspoon salt
75 gm shredded suet
about 120 ml cold water

Grease a 1½ or 2 pint (1 litre) pudding basin. Cut the steak and kidney into ½ inch (1.25 cm) cubes, removing any fat and the core from the kidney. Toss in the flour with the onion, mushrooms and seasoning.

Now prepare the pastry: put the flour, salt and suet in a bowl and mix with the water to a soft but not sticky dough. Cut off a third of the dough and roll out into a circle the size of the top of the basin for a lid. Roll out the remainder and line the basin.

Fill the basin with the meat mixture and add sufficient stock to come three quarters of the way up the meat. Damp the edges of the pastry and cover with the lid, sealing firmly. Cover the pudding with a piece of greased greasproof paper with a pleat in it and a lid of foil.

Cook either by boiling in the normal way for 3½ to 4 hours, topping up with boiling water when necessary, or in a slow cooker on high for 5 hours. The pudding may also be cooked in a pressure cooker: stand the basin on the trivet with 1½ pints (1 litre) boiling water and a spoonful of vinegar. Seal the cooker, wait for a steady flow of steam and then steam gently for 15 minutes. Raise the heat, bring to 5 lb (2.3 kg) pressure and cook for 60 minutes. Then allow the pressure to reduce at room temperature. Serves 4.

Marvellous on a really cold wintry day. It is easy to keep the pudding hot — just leave it standing in a pan of gently simmering water.

French country casserole or pie

1 oz dripping
6 oz streaky bacon, rinded and cut in strips
1½ lb thin flank cut in 1 inch cubes
1 oz flour
½ pint stock
¼ pint red wine
1 bayleaf
sprig of parsley
good pinch mixed dried herbs or a small bunch of fresh herbs
1 level teaspoon salt
good pinch pepper
¼ lb small onions, peeled
7½ oz packet puff pastry, optional

25 gm dripping
175 gm streaky bacon, rinded and cut in strips
675 gm thin flank cut in 2.5 cm cubes
25 gm flour
300 ml stock
150 ml red wine
1 bayleaf
sprig of parsley
good pinch mixed dried herbs or bunch of fresh herbs
1 level teaspoon salt
good pinch pepper
100 gm small onions, peeled
212 gm packet puff pastry, optional

Heat the oven to 325°F, 160°C, Gas No. 3. Melt the dripping in a frying pan and fry the bacon until it begins to brown. Lift out with a slotted spoon and place in a 3 pint (1.7 litre) ovenproof casserole. Fry the meat in the fat remaining in the pan until brown all over, lift out with the spoon and add to the

bacon. Pour off all but 2 table-spoons of fat, stir in the flour and cook until browned. Add the stock and wine and bring to the boil, stirring all the time, then simmer for 2 minutes or until thickened. Add the bayleaf, parsley, herbs and seasoning and pour over the meat. Cover and cook in the oven for 1½ hours. Add the onions and cook for a further hour or until the meat is tender. Remove the parsley, bay-leaf and bunch of herbs, taste and adjust seasoning. If making pie, turn the mixture into a 1½ pint (1 litre) pie dish and leave to become quite cold. Roll out the pastry and use to cover pie, re-roll any trim-mings and cut into leaves to decorate the top. Make a small hole in the centre and brush with a little milk or beaten egg. Bake in a hot oven at 425°F, 220°C, Gas No. 7 for about 30 minutes until the pastry is golden brown and well risen and the meat is hot through. Serves 4 to 6 for the casserole or 6 to 8 for the pie.

An ideal opportunity to use an inex-pensive cut of beef like thin flank, but remember to removed excess fat and skin first.

Spicy beef cassoulet

Sauce:
a few drops of Tobasco sauce
8 oz can peeled tomatoes
¼ pint stock
2 tablespoons soft brown sugar
¼ lb sliced mushrooms
2 tablespoons cider vinegar
2 cloves garlic, crushed
1 bayleaf
1 red pepper

4 oz dried red kidney beans
2 good pinches of bicarbonate of soda
1 oz flour
1 teaspoon salt
good pinch pepper
2 good pinches ground ginger
1½ lb shin of beef cut in 1 inch cubes
2 oz lard or dripping

Sauce:
a few drops Tobasco sauce
225 gm can peeled tomatoes
150 ml stock
2 tablespoons soft brown sugar
100 gm sliced mushrooms
2 tablespoons cider vinegar
2 cloves garlic, crushed
1 bayleaf
1 red pepper

100 gm dried red kidney beans
2 good pinches bicarbonate of soda
25 gm flour
1 teaspoon salt
good pinch pepper
2 good pinches ground ginger
675 gm shin of beef cut in 2.5 cm cubes
50 gm lard or dripping

The red beans in this casserole must be soaked otherwise they are not soft enough to eat. The bicarbonate of soda speeds up the process but is not essential. If you are in a hurry use a 16 oz (450 gm) can of red kidney beans. This is an excellent dish for in-formal entertaining and delicious with a green salad.

Place the kidney beans in a basin with bicarbonate of soda, cover with cold water and leave to stand overnight; drain. Heat the oven to 325°F, 160°C, Gas No. 3. Mix the flour, seasoning and ginger to-gether and coat the meat thorough-ly; melt the dripping in a frying pan and fry the meat quickly to brown, then place in a 3 pint (1.7 litre) casserole with the beans. Combine all the sauce ingredients, except the red pepper, in the pan and bring to the boil. Pour this over the meat, cover and cook in the oven for about 2-3 hours.

Remove the seeds and white pith from the red pepper and cut into rings. Add to the casserole and return to the oven and cook for a further 30 minutes or until the beef is tender. Taste, adjust seasoning and remove the bayleaf.
Serves 4 to 6.

15

Lasagne

Meat Sauce:
1 tablespoon oil
1 lb raw minced beef
1 oz streaky bacon, derinded
   and chopped
8 oz onions, chopped
4 sticks celery, chopped
½ oz flour
½ pint water
3½ oz can tomato purée
2 cloves garlic, crushed
2 teaspoons redcurrant jelly
1 beef stock cube
½ teaspoon salt
pepper
¼ teaspoon dried mixed herbs

White Sauce:
1½ oz butter
1½ oz flour
¼ teaspoon nutmeg
salt and pepper
1 pint milk
½ teaspoon mustard
4 oz Cheddar, grated
4 oz Emmenthal, grated
½ oz Parmesan, grated
5 oz uncooked lasagne pasta

Meat sauce:
15 ml oil
450 gm raw minced beef
25 gm streaky bacon, derinded
   and chopped
225 gm onions, chopped
4 sticks celery, chopped
12.5 gm flour
300 ml water
90 gm can tomato purée
2 cloves garlic, crushed

2 teaspoons redcurrant jelly
1 beef stock cube
pinch salt
pepper
pinch dried mixed herbs

White sauce:
40 gm butter
40 gm flour
pinch nutmeg
salt and pepper
500 ml milk
a little mustard
120 gm Cheddar, grated
120 gm Emmenthal, grated
12 gm Parmesan, grated
150 gm uncooked lasagne pasta

No need to cook the pasta first for this lasagne.

For the meat sauce: heat oil in a pan, add the beef and bacon and fry until browned. Add onions and celery and cook for 5 minutes. Stir in the flour and the remaining sauce ingredients, stir well and bring to the boil. Cover and simmer for 1 hour.

For the white sauce: melt the butter in a large pan and stir in the flour, nutmeg, salt and pepper and cook gently for 2 minutes. Remove the pan from the heat and gradually add the milk, stirring to make a smooth mixture. Return the pan to the heat and cook, stirring until the sauce has thickened. Add mustard and check seasoning. Combine Cheddar and Emmenthal.

In a shallow 3½ pint (2 litre) casserole put a third of the meat sauce, the white sauce and a third of the cheese, followed by half of the uncooked lasagne (lay edge to edge, not overlapping). Then start again with a third of the meat sauce, white sauce and cheese and last half of lasagne. Repeat, finishing with final layer of meat sauce, white sauce and cheese and the grated Parmesan. Leave to become cold, then cook at 350°F, 180°C, Gas No. 4 for about 45 minutes to 1 hour or until the top is browned and bubbling. Serve at once or keep hot at 200°F, 100°C, Gas No. ¼ for up to 1 hour if necessary. Serves 6.

Moussaka

1 small shoulder of lamb, minced
   (this gives about 1 – 1½ lbs
   minced meat)
½ lb onions, chopped
2 cloves garlic, crushed
1½ oz flour
1½ level teaspoons salt
ground black pepper
1 level teaspoon coriander seeds,
   crushed
a little fresh thyme or ¼ teaspoon
   dried thyme
14 oz can tomatoes
4 aubergines

Sauce:
1½ oz butter
1½ oz flour
¾ pint milk
1 level teaspoon made English
   mustard
grated nutmeg
salt and pepper
6 oz mature Cheddar cheese,
   grated
1 egg, beaten
chopped parsley

1 small shoulder of lamb, minced
(this gives about 550 – 700 gm
minced meat)

225 gm onions, chopped
2 cloves garlic, crushed
40 gm flour
generous pinch salt
ground black pepper
generous pinch coriander seeds,
    crushed
a little fresh thyme or pinch
    dried thyme
400 gm can tomatoes
4 aubergines

Sauce:
40 gm butter
40 gm flour
450 ml milk
1 level teaspoon made English
    mustard
grated nutmeg
salt and pepper
175 gm mature Cheddar cheese,
    grated
1 egg, beaten
chopped parsley

In this recipe the aubergines are blanched in water instead of being fried. This is far nicer, I think, than the traditional method and not nearly so fatty.

Heat the oven to 375°F, 190°C, Gas No. 5. Butter a large oven-proof dish, 3 pint (1.5 litre) or larger.

Turn the minced lamb into a large pan, cook over a low heat at first to let the fat run out from the meat and stir to prevent sticking. When the fat has run freely from the meat add the onions and garlic and increase the heat. Fry to brown the meat for about 15 minutes. If there seems to be an excess of fat, spoon off the surplus. Add flour, stir well, then add salt, pepper, coriander, thyme and contents of can of tomatoes. Bring to the boil and simmer for 5 minutes. Check seasoning.

Slice the aubergines into about ¼ inch (0.60 cm) slices and blanch.

in a pan of boiling water for 1 minute. This softens the skin and prevents the aubergines discolouring. Drain in a colander, then dry on kitchen paper.

Make the sauce by slowly melting the butter in a pan, add the flour and cook together for a few minutes over a medium heat without colouring. Blend in the milk, slowly at first, and bring to the boil, stirring well. Add mustard, nutmeg, salt, pepper and cheese. Cook to let the cheese melt then remove from heat. Cool slightly and add the egg, mix well.

Now assemble the moussaka. First put a layer of half the meat mixture in the dish, cover with half the aubergines, season and then repeat with the rest of the lamb and aubergines, so that you end up with 4 layers. Pour over the cheese sauce.

Bake uncovered for 45 minutes to 1 hour until the moussaka is golden brown. Sprinkle with chopped parsley and serve with hot French bread. Serves 6 to 8.

Lamb hot pot

2 lb middle neck or scrag end of
    lamb or 1 lb neck fillet
2 lamb's kidneys
2 lb potatoes, sliced
2 onions, sliced
2 oz mushrooms, sliced
salt and pepper
about ¼ pint stock or water
butter

900 gm middle neck or scrag end
    of lamb or 450 gm neck fillet
2 lamb's kidneys
900 gm potatoes, sliced
2 onions, sliced
50 gm mushrooms
salt and pepper
about 150 ml stock or water
butter

Heat the oven to 350°F, 180°C, Gas No. 4.

Trim the meat, removing the spinal cord and any excess fat, and cut into convenient sized pieces. Halve the kidneys and remove the core and skin, then cut into slices.

Layer the potato with the vegetables, lamb and kidneys in a large 4 to 5 pint (2.3 to 2.8 litre) casserole, seasoning well and finishing with a layer of potatoes arranged neatly on top.

Pour over the stock or water and dot the potatoes with a little butter. Cover and bake in the oven for 1 hour, remove the lid and continue baking for a further 30 to 45 minutes to brown the potatoes. Serves 4.

If your family can't cope with bones in their meat use 1 lb (450 gm) neck fillet of lamb. This is completely boneless, and you won't need such a large casserole.

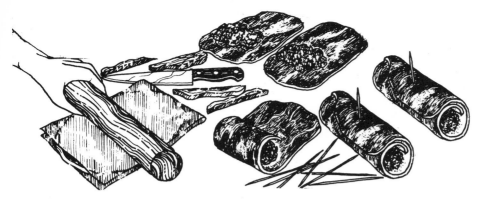

Braised beef olives

4 slices silverside of beef

Stuffing:
1 oz butter
2 oz bacon, chopped
2 oz mushrooms, chopped
2 oz fresh white breadcrumbs
1 level tablespoon chopped
 parsley
salt and ground black pepper

Sauce:
1 oz dripping
1 oz flour
½ pint stock
2 tablespoons sherry
6 sticks celery, sliced
a little gravy browning

4 slices silverside of beef

Stuffing:
25 gm butter
50 gm bacon, chopped
50 gm mushrooms, chopped
50 gm fresh white breadcrumbs
**1 level tablespoon chopped
 parsley**
salt and ground black pepper

Sauce:
25 gm dripping
25 gm flour
300 ml stock
30 ml sherry
6 sticks celery, sliced
a little gravy browning

Trim the meat and then place each piece in turn between wetted greaseproof paper and beat flat with a rolling pin — the wetted paper helps to prevent the meat sticking to the rolling pin.

Prepare the stuffing: melt the butter in a small pan and fry the bacon and mushrooms gently for 2 to 3 minutes, stir in the breadcrumbs, parsley and seasoning and mix well. Divide the stuffing into four and place one portion on each slice of meat, roll up and tie neatly with fine string or fix with cocktail sticks.

Melt the dripping in a frying pan and fry the beef olives to brown on all sides, lift out of the pan and place in the slow cooker. Stir the flour into the fat remaining in the pan and cook for 2 to 3 minutes. Add the stock and sherry and bring to the boil, stirring until thickened, add the celery and plenty of seasoning and a little gravy browning if necessary. Pour over the olives in the slow cooker, cover and cook on high for 30 minutes then turn to low and cook for a further 6 hours. The olives may also be cooked in the oven at 325°F, 160°C, Gas No. 3 for about 2 ½ to 3 hours.

When cooked, lift out the beef olives, remove the string or cocktail sticks and arrange on a serving dish, then spoon over the sauce. Serves 4.

A slow cooker is perfect for this recipe as it needs long slow cooking to make the beef really tender.

Lamb boulangère

1 small leg of lamb
2 cloves garlic
sprig of fresh rosemary
1 ½ lb potatoes
½ lb onions
salt and pepper
½ pint stock
a little chopped parsley

1 small leg of lamb
2 cloves garlic
sprig of fresh rosemary
675 gm potatoes
225 gm onions
salt and pepper
300 ml stock
a little chopped parsley

Preheat the oven — 375°F/190°C/ Gas No. 5.

Trim any excess fat from the lamb. Peel the garlic, cut it into thin slivers and insert them into the lamb. Tie the sprig of rosemary over the lamb.

Peel the potatoes and cut into thick slices. Peel and thinly slice the onions, mix with potatoes, lay in a shallow ovenproof dish and season well. Place the lamb on top and pour over the stock. Cover with a piece of foil and roast in the oven for 30 minutes to the lb (450 gm) and 30 minutes over. After the first hour, remove the foil, baste the meat and vegetables and put in the prepared carrots.

When cooked, untie the rosemary and lay a fresh sprig in its place. Sprinkle the vegetables with a little chopped parsley and serve in the dish in which the meal has been cooked. Serves 6 to 8.

Vichy carrots

1½ lb carrots
½ pint stock or water
1 oz butter
salt and pepper

675 gm carrots
300 ml stock or water
25 gm butter
salt and pepper

Peel the carrots and cut lengthwise into strips. Put in a 2 pint (good 1 litre) ovenproof casserole and add the stock or water, butter and seasoning. Cover with a well-fitting lid or a piece of foil and bake in the oven with the lamb for 1½ hours or until tender. Serve with a little of the cooking liquor. Serves 6.

Use this recipe and make your complete meal in the oven. Serve casseroled carrots cooked in butter and stock to accompany the lamb, and for pudding perhaps a fruit crumble.

Liver in onion sauce

1 lb pig's or lamb's liver
½ lb onions
2 oz dripping
2 oz flour
1 pint beef stock or 1 pint water
    and 1 beef stock cube
3 tablespoons tomato ketchup
pinch dried marjoram
a few drops of Worcester sauce
salt and pepper

450 gm pig's or lamb's liver
225 gm onions
50 gm dripping
50 gm flour
600 ml beef stock or 600 ml
    water and 1 beef stock cube
3 tablespoons tomato ketchup
pinch dried marjoram
a few drops of Worcester sauce
salt and pepper

Cut the liver into long strips about ½ inch (1.25 cm) wide, then soak in milk for 30 minutes; drain off milk and discard.

Peel and slice the onions. Melt the dripping in a pan, add the onions and fry for 5 to 10 minutes until the onions are golden brown. Stir in the flour and cook for 2 minutes, add the stock and bring to the boil, stirring until thickened. Add ketchup, marjoram, Worcester sauce and seasoning, stir well and cover pan. Reduce heat and simmer for 20 minutes.

Add liver to sauce and cook for about 10 minutes. Serves 5.

If you don't like the stronger flavour of pig's liver but find lamb's liver too dear, then soak it in milk before cooking. This is a moist and flavoursome way of cooking it and your family will find it hard to tell the difference.

Bacon-stuffed hearts

4 lamb's hearts

Stuffing:
¼ lb streaky bacon
1 onion
3 oz cooked rice (1 oz raw rice)
1 level tablespoon chopped
  parsley
salt and pepper

Sauce:
10½ oz can condensed tomato
  soup
1 level tablespoon redcurrant jelly

4 lamb's hearts

Stuffing:
100 gm streaky bacon
1 onion
75 gm cooked rice (25 gm raw
  rice)
1 level teaspoon chopped parsley
salt and pepper

Sauce:
298 gm can condensed tomato
  soup
1 level tablespoon redcurrant
  jelly

Wash the hearts well and cut away the tubes.

Remove the rind and bone from the bacon and cut into strips. Peel and finely chop the onion and fry with the bacon for about 5 minutes so that the fat comes out of the bacon. Stir in the rice, parsley and seasoning. Divide the stuffing between the hearts, pressing firmly into the cavities, and secure with wooden cocktail sticks.

Place the hearts in a deep ovenproof casserole, pour over the soup and stir in the redcurrant jelly. Cover with a lid or a piece of foil and bake in a moderate oven at 325°F, 160°C, Gas No. 3 for 1¾ hours or until the hearts are tender. Remove the cocktail sticks before serving. Serves 4.

Rice is an ideal accompaniment to this dish and helps to sop up the delicious sauce.

Oxtail

1 oxtail, jointed, about 2½ lb in
  weight
1½ oz dripping
1 oz flour
1 pint water
1 beef stock cube
2 onions, chopped
2 carrots, chopped
2 sticks celery, sliced
salt and pepper
pinch of cayenne pepper
1 bayleaf
a little gravy browning

1 oxtail, jointed, about 1 kg in
  weight
40 gm dripping
25 gm flour
600 ml water
1 beef stock cube
2 onions, chopped
2 carrots, chopped
2 sticks celery, sliced
salt and pepper
pinch cayenne pepper
1 bayleaf
a little gravy browning

Trim any excess fat from the oxtail. Heat the dripping in a large pan and fry the oxtail quickly on all sides to brown; remove from the pan. Stir the flour into the fat remaining in the pan and cook for a minute, then stir in the water and bring to the boil, add the stock cube and stir until dissolved.

Return the oxtail to the pan with the vegetables, seasoning and bay leaf, cover and simmer very gently for 3½ to 4 hours until the meat can be easily removed from the bones. Skim off any surplus fat, remove the bayleaf.

Adjust the seasoning and add a little gravy browning. Turn into a dish and serve. Serves 4 to 6.

Make sure to trim off excess fat from the joints. If the oxtail is cooked the day before it is required, leave it to cool completely before removing fat.

Danish meatballs

8 oz lean minced beef
8 oz lean minced pork
1 oz flour
1 egg, beaten
1 teaspoon salt
ground black pepper
pinch grated nutmeg

Sauce:
1½ oz dripping
12 oz onions, chopped
1½ oz flour
¾ pint dry cider
1 beef stock cube
salt and pepper
a little browning to colour

225 gm lean minced beef
225 gm lean minced pork
25 gm flour
1 egg, beaten
1 teaspoon salt
ground black pepper
pinch grated nutmeg

Sauce:
40 gm dripping
350 gm onions, chopped
40 gm flour
450 ml dry cider
1 beef stock cube
salt and pepper
a little browning to colour

Mix the beef, pork, flour, egg, seasoning and nutmeg together thoroughly and shape into 8 even-sized balls.

Melt the dripping in a saucepan and fry the meat balls quickly until brown all over, lift out with a slotted spoon and keep on one side. Add the onions to the dripping remaining in the pan and fry quickly to brown. Stir in the flour and cook gently until starting to turn brown. Add the cider, stock cube and seasoning and bring to the boil, stirring until thickened. If necessary add a little browning to the sauce. Return the meat balls to the pan, cover and simmer gently for 30 to 45 minutes.

Alternatively, the meat balls may be put in a casserole, covered and cooked in a moderate oven 350°F, 180°C, Gas No. 4 for about 1 to 1¼ hours. Serves 4.

These are meat balls in a rich onion sauce, good enough to serve for a supper party. Serve with buttered noodles with added ground black pepper.

Homemade beefburgers with barbecue sauce

¾ lb best minced beef
¼ lb pork sausagemeat
1 medium onion, grated
1 level teaspoon salt
ground black pepper

Barbecue sauce:
2 oz butter
1 medium onion, finely chopped
8 tablespoons tomato ketchup
4 tablespoons vinegar
4 tablespoons mango chutney, chopped
½ level teaspoon French mustard
2 teaspoons castor sugar
2 tablespoons Worcestershire sauce

350 gm best minced beef
100 gm pork sausagemeat
1 medium onion, grated
1 level teaspoon salt
ground black pepper

Barbecue sauce:
50 gm butter
1 medium onion, finely chopped
8 tablespoons tomato ketchup
60 ml vinegar
4 tablespoons mango chutney, chopped
scant teaspoon French mustard
2 teaspoons castor sugar
30 ml Worcestershire sauce

You could add a teaspoon of chopped fresh herbs if liked. These beefburgers freeze well raw and should be used within 6 weeks if kept in the freezer.

Place the minced beef, sausagemeat, onion, salt and plenty of ground black pepper in a bowl and blend well together. Flour your hands and roll the mixture into 8 balls and flatten each out to a 3 inch (7.5 cm) beefburger. Grill or fry in a very little dripping for about 2½ minutes on each side.

To make the sauce: melt the butter in a small pan and fry the onion gently until tender without colouring. Add the remaining ingredients and bring to the boil and simmer for 2 minutes.

Serve the sauce either hot or cold; if any should be left over it may be stored in the refrigerator for up to 3 weeks. Serves 4.

Chicken

Avocado and chicken mayonnaise

3 ½ lb chicken, roasted
1 large avocado pear
¼ pint mayonnaise
salt
freshly ground black pepper
1 teaspoon lemon juice
lettuce, tomato slices and parsley
    to garnish

1.5 kg chicken, roasted
1 large avocado pear
150 ml mayonnaise
salt
freshly ground black pepper
5 ml lemon juice
lettuce, tomato slices and parsley
    to garnish

Cut the chicken into bite-size pieces, removing all skin and bones.

Cut the avocado in half and remove the stone. Scoop out the flesh and chop roughly. Mash half the avocado and mix with the mayonnaise, salt, pepper and lemon juice until smooth. This can be done in a blender. Turn into a bowl and stir in the remaining avocado and the chicken. Serves 4 to 6.

To serve, arrange on a bed of lettuce hearts spoon the mixture into the centre and garnish.

Mayonnaise
2 egg yolks
1 level teaspoon made mustard
1 level teaspoon salt
⅛ level teaspoon white pepper
1 level teaspoon castor sugar
1 tablespoon white wine or
    cider vinegar
½ pint vegetable or corn oil
1 tablespoon lemon juice

2 egg yolks
1 level teaspoon made mustard
1 level teaspoon salt
pinch of white pepper
1 level teaspoon castor sugar
15 ml white wine or cider
    vinegar
300 ml vegetable or corn oil
15 ml lemon juice

Stand a bowl on a damp cloth to prevent it slipping on the table. Put yolks, mustard, salt, pepper and sugar into the bowl with vinegar and mix well. Add the oil drop by drop, beating well with a whisk the whole time until the mixture is smooth and thick. Beat in the lemon juice.

In order that the oil may be added a drop at a time, put into the bottle-neck a cork from which a small wedge has been cut. Makes ½ pint mayonnaise.

Devilled chicken

salt and ground black pepper
4 thigh roasting joints of chicken

Sauce:
1 rounded tablespoon apricot jam
1 teaspoon Dijon mustard
pinch cayenne pepper
large clove garlic, crushed
1 tablespoon Worcestershire sauce
3 tablespoons tomato ketchup
1 tablespoon soy sauce

salt and ground black pepper
4 thigh roasting joints of chicken

Sauce:
1 rounded tablespoon apricot jam
1 teaspoon Dijon mustard
pinch cayenne pepper
large clove garlic, crushed
1 tablespoon Worcestershire sauce
3 tablespoons tomato ketchup
1 tablespoon soy sauce

Heat oven to 350°F, 180°C, Gas No. 4.

Season the chicken joints well on all sides and put in a shallow ovenproof dish so that they just touch.

Measure the jam into a basin, add mustard, cayenne, garlic and Worcestershire sauce, blend well until smooth. Then add the other ingredients, season with black pepper and a little salt and pour over the chicken, coating evenly.

Bake for about 1 hour at the top of the oven. To test when done prod the thickest part of the thigh with a fine skewer. If the juices run out clear the chicken is done, if pink give the chicken a little longer.

Serve with spicy rice and a green salad. Serves 4.

For a delicious supper serve devilled chicken with mild spicy rice.

Paprika chicken

4 chicken breasts
2 tablespoons salad oil
1 oz butter
1 onion, chopped
2 level tablespoons paprika pepper
1 oz flour
¼ pint stock
¼ pint dry cider
5 tablespoons sherry
1 level teaspoon tomato puree
salt and pepper
6 oz small button mushrooms
¼ pint soured cream
chopped parsley
fried sliced mushrooms

4 chicken breasts
2 tablespoons salad oil
25 gm butter
1 onion, chopped
2 level tablespoons paprika pepper
25 gm flour
150 ml stock
150 ml dry cider
5 tablespoons sherry
1 level teaspoon tomato puree
salt and pepper
175 gm small button mushrooms
150 ml soured cream
chopped parsley
fried sliced mushrooms

Remove the skin from the chicken breasts. Heat the oil in a large shallow pan, add the butter and then fry the chicken quickly to slightly brown. Remove from the pan and drain on kitchen paper. Add the onion and paprika to the pan and fry for 2 minutes. Blend in the flour and cook for a further minute. Remove from the heat and stir in the stock, cider and sherry. Return to the heat and simmer until thick. Add the tomato puree and seasoning to the sauce, stir well and then return the chicken breasts to the pan; cover and simmer gently for 30 minutes, turning once.

Wash the mushrooms, add to the pan and simmer for a further 5 minutes.

When ready to serve, lift the chicken breasts onto a serving dish and stir the soured cream over the chicken. Sprinkle with parsley and garnish the dish with fried sliced mushrooms. Serves 4.

A rich creamy chicken dish delicious with rice, noodles or new potatoes and a green salad or broccoli.

Quick chicken pie

Shortcrust pastry:
4 oz plain flour
1 oz lard
1 oz margarine
1 tablespoon cold water

Filling:
8 oz cooked chicken.
4 oz cooked ham
10½ oz can condensed
    mushroom soup

Shortcrust pastry:
100 gm plain flour
25 gm lard
25 gm margarine
15 ml cold water

Filling:
225 gm cooked chicken
100 gm cooked ham
300 gm can condensed
    mushroom soup

Heat the oven to 400°F, 200°C, Gas No. 6.

Sift the flour into a bowl and add the fats cut into small pieces. Rub in with the fingertips until the mixture resembles fine breadcrumbs. Add the water and work in with a fork or knife to make a firm dough. Wrap and chill in the fridge for half an hour.

Cut the chicken and ham into small pieces. Mix well with the soup and turn into a 1 pint (600 ml) pie dish. Brush the edges of the dish with a little milk, roll out the pastry on a floured table and cover the pie dish. Use any trimmings left to make leaves for decoration. Brush with a little milk, make two slits in the top of the pie and bake for 30 minutes until golden brown. Serves 3 to 4.

Even quicker if you prepare the pastry in advance — the pastry mixture can be stored up to 6 weeks in the refrigerator when at the breadcrumb stage, and for up to 3 months in the freezer.

Mild chicken curry with cream and grapes

3 lb chicken
2 small onions, peeled
2 cloves
1 bayleaf
parsley
1 level teaspoon salt
6 peppercorns
½ pint water
½ pint sweet cider
¼ lb white grapes
1 oz butter
1 level teaspoon curry powder
1 oz flour
2 teaspoons redcurrant jelly
¼ pint single cream
salt and pepper
watercress

1.3 kg chicken
2 small onions, peeled
2 cloves
1 bayleaf
parsley
1 level teaspoon salt
6 peppercorns
300 ml water
300 ml sweet cider
100 gm white grapes
25 gm butter
1 level teaspoon curry powder
25 gm flour
2 teaspoons redcurrant jelly
150 ml single cream
salt and pepper
watercress

Place the chicken in a pan with the onions stuck with cloves, bayleaf, parsley, salt and peppercorns. Pour over the water and cider, cover the pan and simmer gently for 1 to 1¼ hours or until the chicken is tender.

While the chicken is cooking, skin and pip most of the grapes and put a few on one side for garnish.

Remove the chicken from the pan and leave to cool. Boil the stock rapidly until reduced to ½ pint (300 ml), strain and put on one side and skim off the surplus fat. Removed the flesh from the chicken, cut into neat pieces, place in a serving dish and keep warm.

Melt the butter in a pan, stir in the curry powder and cook gently for 2 minutes. Stir in the flour and cook for a minute. Slowly blend in the stock and bring to the boil, stirring. Add the redcurrant jelly and simmer for 2 to 3 minutes, season well and add the halved grapes.

Remove the sauce from the heat and stir in the cream. Coat the chicken with the sauce and garnish the dish with small sprigs of watercress and the remaining grapes.

Serve with boiled rice and a green salad. Serves 4 to 6.

This old favourite of mine is perfect for a summer dinner party being light and mildly curry flavoured.

Chicken galantine

3½ lb chicken
12 oz lean pork, minced
12 oz pork sausagemeat
1 small onion, minced
2 cloves garlic, crushed
1½ oz fresh breadcrumbs
1 egg
large pinch dried thyme
1 teaspoon salt
plenty of ground black pepper
4 oz slice cooked ham
1 oz green stuffed olives

1.5 kg chicken
350 gm lean pork
350 gm pork sausagemeat
1 small onion, minced
2 cloves garlic, crushed
40 gm fresh breadcrumbs
1 egg
large pinch dried thyme
1 teaspoon salt
plenty of ground black pepper
100 gm slice cooked ham
25 gm green stuffed olives

Bone the chicken. Make a cut along the length of the backbone and with a small sharp knife cut the flesh away from the bones down each side. When you come to the wing knuckle cut it away from the carcass. Scrape the meat off the bone down to the first joint. Cut off there and then repeat with the other side.

With the leg joint, cut away again at the carcass, but scrape the meat away from the two bones of the leg, turning the flesh inside out as you go. Carefully cut the meat away from the rest of the carcass until you can lift it out. Remove any excess lumps of fat and lay the chicken skin-side down on a board, tuning the legs back ito shape. Use the carcass for making stock or soup.

Heat the oven to 375°F, 190°C, Gas No. 5.

Mix together the pork sausage meat, onion, garlic, breadcrumbs, egg, thyme and salt and pepper. Spread half this mixture down the centre of the chicken.

Cut the ham into ¾ inch (2 cm) strips lengthwise and lay on top of the stuffing interspersed with the olives. Cover with the remaining pork mixture and wrap the chicken over. Turn over and shape to resemble a chicken, place in a meat roasting tin and very lightly spread the breast with a little butter.

Bake in the centre of the oven for 1½ hours, basting occasionally.

Lift out and place on a dish to cool. When quite cold put in the refrigerator until required. Then serve sliced with various salads. Serves 10.

Although this takes time to do it is worth it for a party. If you give your butcher lots of warning he may well bone the chicken for you.

Chicken in cider with mushrooms

3½ lb chicken
½ pint dry cider
1 onion, chopped
ground black pepper
salt
milk
2 oz butter
2 oz flour
½ lb button mushrooms, sliced
chopped parsley and croutons
    to garnish

1.5 kg chicken
300 ml dry cider
1 onion, chopped
ground black pepper
salt
milk
50 gm butter
50 gm flour
225 gm button mushrooms,
    sliced
chopped parsley and croutons
    to garnish

Put the chicken and the giblets in a small roasting tin or casserole, add the cider and chopped onions, season well. Cover with a lid or a piece of foil and cook at 350°F, 180°C, Gas No. 4 for 20 minutes to the lb (450 gm) and 20 minutes over — i.e., about 1½ hours. Test to see if it is cooked by piercing the thickest part of the leg with a skewer; if the juices come out clear the bird is cooked. Lift the chicken out to cool and strain off the remaining liquid in the tin, skim off the fat and make up to 1¼ pints (750 ml) with milk.

Keep the liver with the chicken and chop. Remove the meat from the bird and cut into good-sized pieces. Use the carcass and the giblets to make stock for soup on another occasion.

Melt the butter for the sauce in a pan and add the flour and cook for 2 minutes without colouring. Stir in the stock and the milk, slowly at first and bring to the boil, add the mushrooms and season with lots of black pepper and salt. Stir in the chicken and turn into an ovenproof serving dish, cool, cover and keep in the refrigerator for up to 24 hours.

To reheat, place in the oven with the potato and onion layer (375°F, 190°C, Gas No. 5) for the last 50 minutes of cooking time.

Sprinkle with chopped parsley and serve garnished with fried bread croutons cut in triangles and a green salad or vegetables. (The croutons may be made early in the day, drained well and put in the oven to reheat for the last 5 minutes of the cooking time.) Serves 6.

For an extra creamy and rich sauce add a couple of tablespoons (30 ml) of soured or thick cream just before serving.

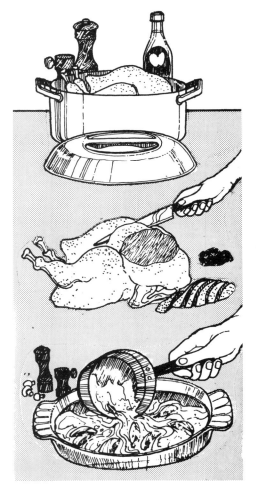

Chicken paella

5 tablespoons oil
1 lb raw chicken on the bone,
  in pieces
8 oz streaky bacon pieces,
  chopped
1 large onion, chopped
2 cloves garlic, crushed
½ lb tomatoes, skinned and
  seeded
1½ pints chicken stock
thimble of saffron powder or
  ½ level teaspoon turmeric
2 level teaspoons salt
plenty of ground black pepper
1 lb long grain refined rice
4 oz peeled prawns
4 oz frozen peas
12 whole prawns in shell
8 oz green pepper, seeded
  and sliced
12 stuffed green olives
wedges of lemon
mussels if liked

75 ml oil
450 gm raw chicken on the bone,
  in pieces
225 gm streaky bacon pieces,
  chopped
1 large onion, chopped
2 cloves garlic, crushed
225 gm tomatoes, skinned
  and seeded
1 litre chicken stock
thimble of saffron powder
  or pinch turmeric
2 level teaspoons salt

plenty of ground black pepper
450 gm long grain refined rice
100 gm peeled prawns
100 gm frozen peas
12 whole prawns in shell
225 gm green pepper, seeded
  and sliced
12 stuffed green olives
wedges of lemon
mussels if liked

Heat the oil in the paella pan, add the chicken and fry over a medium heat for about 15 minutes, turning until brown on all sides. Add the bacon and onion and fry for a further 5 minutes.

Stir in the garlic, tomatoes, stock and saffron and bring to the boil, add the salt and pepper and stir in the rice, peeled prawns and peas.

Arrange the whole prawns and green pepper slices on top.

Cover with a lid if you have one to fit, or with foil. Transfer to the oven and cook at 350°F, 180°C, Gas No. 4 for about 45 minutes or until the rice is tender and the stock is absorbed. Taste and check seasoning and decorate with cooked mussels, stuffed green olives and wedges of lemon if liked. Serves 8.

Paella makes a very good party dish. It is traditionally cooked in a round pan with two handles called a paellera, but at home I use an old frying pan with short metal handles or a shallow flameproof dish. If liked add some fresh cooked mussels.

Roast chicken with apricot and nut stuffing

2 oz dried apricots
1 oz butter
1 onion, chopped
2 oz brown breadcrumbs
1 oz peanuts or cashew nuts
  coarsely chopped

grated rind of ½ a lemon
1 level teaspoon brown sugar
1 rounded tablespoon chopped
  parsley
salt and pepper
3½ lb chicken

50 gm dried apricots
25 gm butter
1 onion, chopped
50 gm brown breadcrumbs
25 gm peanuts or cashew nuts,
  coarsely chopped
grated rind of ½ a lemon
1 level teaspoon brown sugar
1 rounded tablespoon chopped
  parsley
salt and pepper
1.5 kg chicken

Place the apricots in a small bowl, cover with water and leave to soak overnight. Drain and place in a saucepan with water just to cover and simmer gently for about 20 minutes until just cooked. Drain well, reserving the juice for making gravy. Leave the apricots to cool, then chop coarsely.

Heat the oven to 375°F, 190°C, Gas No. 5.

Melt the butter in a pan, add the onion and cook gently for about 10 minutes or until soft, but not brown, then stir in the apricots, breadcrumbs, nuts, lemon rind, sugar, parsley and plenty of seasoning. Mix thoroughly and use to stuff the neck end of the chicken.

Place the chicken in a roasting tin, cover the breast with a little butter and roast in the centre of the oven for about 1½ hours or until tender. When the thickest part of the leg is pricked with a skewer the juices will run clear.

Serve with a gravy made using the apricot juice. Serves 6.

Don't chop the nuts too finely for this recipe. Brown breadcrumbs make a change from white and add to the flavour too.

Vegetables

French vegetable quiche

6 oz plain flour
4 oz butter
1½ oz Parmesan cheese
1 tablespoon cold water
1 egg yolk

Filling:
1 oz butter
1 oz flour
½ pint milk
1 level teaspoon made mustard
3 oz grated Cheddar cheese
salt and pepper
¾ lb cooked mixed vegetables
  (e.g. leeks, carrots, peas, beans;
  not cabbage or sprouts)
chopped parsley

175 gm plain flour
100 gm butter
40 gm Parmesan cheese
15 ml cold water
1 egg yolk

Filling:
25 gm butter
25 gm flour
300 ml milk
1 level teaspoon made mustard
75 gm grated Cheddar
salt and pepper
350 gm cooked mixed vegetables
  (e.g. leeks, carrots, peas, beans;
  not cabbage or sprouts)
chopped parsley

Sift the flour into a bowl. Add the butter cut in small pieces and rub in with the fingertips until the mixture resembles fine breadcrumbs. Stir in the Parmesan cheese. Blend the water with the egg yolk, add to the flour and mix to a firm dough. Roll out on a lightly floured table and line a 9 inch (22.5 cm) flan tin. Chill for 15 minutes.

Heat the oven to 425°F, 220°C, Gas No. 7. Put in a baking sheet to warm. Line the flan with a piece of greaseproof paper and weigh down with baking beans. Bake blind for 20 to 25 minutes until pastry is golden brown at the edges and crisp.

Meanwhile melt the butter for the filling in a saucepan and stir in the flour. Cook for 2 minutes. Gradually add the milk and bring to the boil, stirring until thickened. Add the mustard, cheese and seasoning.

Cut the vegetables into even sized pieces and add to the sauce. Re-heat thoroughly and then spoon into the flan case. Sprinkle with parsley and serve. Serves 6.

This makes a very good family supper dish and is an excellent way of using up a selection of leftover vegetables, as long as they are barely tender. Make the flan case in advance and warm it through in the oven to crispen the pastry before filling with the vegetables and sauce. For extra hungry guests you could add chopped cooked ham or garnish the flan with bacon rolls.

Chipped potatoes

old potatoes
oil for frying

Peel the potatoes and cut into ¼ to ½ inch (5 mm to 1.25 cm) slices. Cut these slices into strips ¼ to ½ inch (5 mm to 1.25 cm) wide.

Wash in cold water, drain and dry thoroughly with a tea towel or on kitchen paper.

Heat the oil to 375°F, 190°C. To test whether the oil is hot enough, drop a chip into it. If it rises to the surface and bubbles, the oil is ready for frying.

Place a layer of chips in a wire basket and lower into the pan. Cook for about 4 minutes or until the chips are just cooked and a very pale golden brown. This is called blanching. Drain thoroughly on kitchen paper and repeat until all the chips have been fried.

Just before serving fry the chips again for a few minutes until golden brown. Drain well and serve, sprinkling with a little salt if liked.

To freeze chips: deep-fat fry the chips in hot oil, 360°F, 185°C, or until just tender but not browned. Drain thoroughly on kitchen paper and cool quickly. Open-freeze then pack into polythene bags, seal, label and return to the freezer. The frying temperature is lower as the chipped potatoes are not browned for freezing. Thaw the chips, turn into hot oil and cook until golden brown. Drain well before serving.

The best potatoes for making chips are Maris Piper main crop potatoes. These are the ones that the best British fish and chip shops use.

Niçoise salad

7 oz can tuna
3 hard-boiled eggs
2 tablespoons coarsely chopped
  parsley
4 firm tomatoes
½ cucumber
8 oz French beans, cooked
  until crisp
2 spring onions, chopped
1 cos or Webb's lettuce
⅛ pint French dressing
2 oz can anchovy fillets

4 firm tomatoes
½ cucumber
225 gm French beans, cooked
  until crisp
2 spring onions, chopped
1 cos or Webb's lettuce
75 ml French dressing
50 gm anchovy fillets
200 gm can tuna
3 hard-boiled eggs
2 tablespoons coarsely chopped
  parsley

Quarter the tomatoes, slice the cucumber, cut the French beans into short lengths and add to the spring onions.

Wash the lettuce, tear into strips and arrange in the bottom of the salad bowl. Thoroughly drain the anchovy fillets and add with the vegetables to the French dressing, toss lightly and spoon over the lettuce.

Drain the tuna fish, lightly flake and place on top of the vegetables. Cut each egg in half lengthwise and arrange around the edge of the salad, sprinkle with parsley and serve. If liked the salad may be tossed lightly to mix all the ingredients together but take care not to over blend or the appearance will be messy. Serves 6.

Cos or Webb's lettuce are perfect for this. Don't use a flabby round lettuce as it does not have the crispness.

Red cabbage

1 medium red
  cabbage
1 lb windfall apples, weight
  after peeling
¼ pint water
1½ oz sugar
1 teaspoon salt
4 cloves
6 tablespoons vinegar
2 oz butter
1 tablespoon redcurrant jelly

1 medium red cabbage
450 gm windfall apples, weight
  after peeling
150 ml water
50 gm sugar
1 teaspoon salt
4 cloves
6 tablespoons vinegar
50 gm butter
1 tablespoon redcurrant jelly

Trim and clean cabbage. Shred finely. Peel, core and slice apples. Place cabbage and apples in a pan

with the water, sugar, salt and cloves. Cover and simmer until tender for about ¾ hour. Remove cloves, add vinegar, butter and jelly. Blend well over the heat. Check seasoning and serve hot with meat dishes. Serves 4.

One of the best and most warming vegetables, it also reheats well, should some be left. Reheat in a nonstick pan, stirring until piping hot.

French onion and bacon flan

Pastry:
6 oz plain flour
pinch salt
1½ oz margarine
1½ oz lard
about 2 tablespoons cold water
   to mix

Filling:
2 oz butter
8 oz onions, thinly sliced
4 oz lean bacon, chopped
2 eggs
½ pint single cream
salt
freshly ground black pepper
2 oz Cheddar cheese, grated

Pastry:
175 gm plain flour
pinch salt
40 gm margarine
40 gm lard
about 30 ml cold water to mix

Filling:
50 gm butter
225 gm onions, thinly sliced
100 gm lean bacon, chopped
2 eggs
300 ml single cream
salt
freshly ground black pepper
50 gm Cheddar cheese, grated

Heat the oven to 425°F, 220°C, Gas No. 7.

Make the pastry in the usual way (see Quick chicken pie) and line an oval dish. Chill in the refrigerator for 10 minutes. Fill with grease-proof paper and baking beans and bake blind for 15 minutes.

Meanwhile prepare the filling: melt the butter in a small saucepan, add the onions and bacon and fry gently for 5 minutes.

Remove the flan from the oven and take out the baking beans and paper. Lift the onions and bacon from the pan with a slotted spoon, drain well and spread over the base of the flan. Blend the eggs with the cream and seasoning and pour into the flan; sprinkle with cheese.

Reduce the oven temperature to 350°F, 180°C, Gas No. 4 and bake the flan for a further 25 to 30 minutes until the filling is set and golden brown. Serves 6.

This flan is delicious served for lunch or supper with a green salad and crusty French bread.

29

Ratatouille

1 green pepper
1 red pepper
4 tablespoons oil
2 Spanish onions, sliced
2 courgettes, sliced
8 oz tomatoes, skinned, quartered and the seeds removed
salt and pepper

1 green pepper
1 red pepper
4 tablespoons oil
2 Spanish onions, sliced
2 courgettes, sliced
225 gm tomatoes, skinned, quartered and the seeds removed
salt and pepper

Remove the seeds and pith from the green and red peppers and cut into strips. Heat the oil in a thick pan and add the peppers and onions, cover and cook slowly for about 20 minutes, stirring occasionally until the onions are soft.

Add the courgettes and tomatoes with plenty of salt and pepper and cook without the lid for a further 10 to 15 minutes or until the courgettes are tender. Serves 4.

Make ratatouille when peppers and courgettes are reasonably priced in the summer. Add garlic as well if you like it. Serve with meat without a sauce such as a roast chicken or grilled fish or chops.

Pissaladière

Pastry:
6 oz plain flour
3 oz unsalted butter
1 egg, beaten
about 1 to 2 tablespoons
   cold water

Filling:
3 tablespoons oil
1 lb onions, finely sliced
2 cloves garlic, crushed
14 oz can tomatoes,
   roughly chopped
1 level tablespoon tomato purée
1 level teaspoon sugar
1 rounded tablespoon chopped
   parsley
½ level teaspoon salt
freshly ground black pepper
3 oz grated Cheddar cheese
1¾ oz can anchovies
12 stuffed green olives

Pastry:
175 gm plain flour
75 gm unsalted butter
1 egg, beaten
about 15 to 30 ml cold water

Filling:
45 ml oil
450 gm onions, finely sliced
2 cloves garlic, crushed
400 gm can tomatoes,
   roughly chopped
1 level tablespoon tomato purée
1 level teaspoon sugar
1 rounded tablespoon chopped
   parsley
scant teaspoon salt
freshly ground black pepper
75 gm grated Cheddar cheese
42 gm can anchovies
12 stuffed green olives

A classic flan from the south of France. It's rather like an Italian pizza but is made with a light scone-crust pastry with added egg; tastiest when served hot as soon as it is baked.

Prepare the pastry: measure flour into a bowl and rub in the butter until the mixture resembles fine breadcrumbs, add the egg and enough cold water to make the pastry come cleanly away from the sides of the bowl. Turn onto a floured table and knead lightly, then roll out and line a 9 inch (22.5 cm) fluted flan ring. Prick the base lightly with a fork, leave to rest for 15 minutes in the refrigerator.

Meanwhile prepare the filling. Heat the oil in a pan and add the onions and garlic, cover and cook over a low heat until soft, stirring occasionally. This will take about 30 minutes. Put the tomatoes in another pan with the purée and sugar and boil rapidly until reduced to about ¼ pint (150 ml). Stir into the onions with the parsley and seasoning, leave to cool.

Heat the oven to 400°F, 200°C,

Gas No. 6 and bake the flan blind for 15 minutes, then remove from the oven and spoon in the filling. Sprinkle with cheese and arrange the anchovies in a lattice pattern on top, placing an olive in each space. Return to the oven and cook for a further 25 minutes until the cheese is just starting to brown. Serves 6.

Stuffed green peppers

4 large even-sized green peppers
3 oz long grain rice
1 oz butter
1 small onion, chopped
4 oz button mushrooms, sliced
4 rashers back bacon, chopped
salt
freshly ground black pepper
1 rounded teaspoon chopped
   parsley
1 egg, beaten

Cheese Sauce:
1 oz butter
1 oz flour
½ pint milk
1 teaspoon made mustard
a little grated nutmeg
salt and pepper
4 oz Cheddar cheese, grated

4 large even-sized green peppers
75 gm long grain rice
25 gm butter
1 small onion, chopped
100 gm button mushrooms,
   sliced
4 rashers back bacon, chopped
salt
freshly ground black pepper
1 rounded teaspoon chopped
   parsley
1 egg, beaten

Cheese sauce:
25 gm butter
25 gm flour
300 ml milk
1 teaspoon made mustard
a little grated nutmeg
salt and pepper
100 gm Cheddar, grated

Cut a circle from the base of each green pepper to remove the stem and seeds.

Cook the rice in boiling salted water for 10 to 12 minutes or until tender, drain and rinse well. Melt the butter in a pan and fry the onion, mushrooms and bacon for 5 minutes. Stir in the cooked rice, salt, plenty of freshly ground black pepper and parsley, then stir in the egg to bind the rice.

Arrange the peppers fairly close together in an ovenproof dish and spoon in the filling. Heat the oven to 350°F, 180°C, Gas No. 4.

Now make the sauce: melt the butter in a small saucepan and add the flour and cook for 1 minute. Add the milk and bring to the boil, stirring, simmer until thickened, add mustard, nutmeg and seasoning and stir in 2 oz (50 gm) of the grated cheese. Pour this sauce around the stuffed peppers. Sprinkle the top of each pepper with the remaining cheese.

Bake in the oven for 45 to 50 minutes or until the peppers are tender. Serves 4.

A good supper dish served with warm crisp fresh bread. Vary the ingredients with the rice according to what you have at hand, perhaps add a couple of chopped chicken livers or ham instead of bacon.

Soufflé omelette

2 large eggs
1 dessertspoon castor sugar
2 teaspoons cold water
½ oz butter
1 rounded tablespoon strawberry
  or black cherry jam
icing sugar

2 large eggs
1 dessertspoon castor sugar
2 teaspoons cold water
12.5 gm butter
1 rounded tablespoon strawberry
  or black cherry jam
icing sugar

Separate the eggs and place the yolks in a basin with the sugar and water, beat until pale and creamy.

Whisk the egg whites using a hand rotary or electric whisk until just stiff. Mix 1 tablespoonful into the yolks and carefully fold in the remainder.

Heat the pan and then melt the butter in it over a moderate heat. Spread the mixture into the pan and cook without moving for 3 to 4 minutes until a pale golden brown underneath.

Slip under a medium grill for 2 to 3 minutes to set the top. Make a slight cut across the centre of the omelette, spread one half with warmed jam, fold in half and slide on to a warm serving plate. Dredge with icing sugar and serve at once. Serves 2.

This is an easy pudding that can quickly be made of ingredients that most of us have to hand.

Lemon soufflé pudding

4 oz butter or margarine, softened
12 oz castor sugar
4 eggs, separated
4 oz self-raising flour
grated rind of 2 large lemons
6 tablespoons lemon juice
1 pint milk

100 gm butter or margarine,
  softened
350 gm castor sugar
4 eggs, separated
100 gm self-raising flour
grated rind of 2 large lemons
6 tablespoons lemon juice
600 ml milk

Heat the oven to 375°F, 190°C, Gas No. 5. Butter well a shallow 3 pint (1.5 litre) ovenproof dish.

Beat the butter or margarine with the sugar until smooth. Beat in the egg yolks, then stir in the flour, lemon rind, juice and milk. Don't worry if the mixture looks curdled at this stage; it is quite normal.

Whisk the egg whites using a hand rotary or electric whisk until they form soft peaks and fold into the lemon mixture. Pour into the prepared dish and place in a meat tin half filled with hot water. Bake for about 1 hour or until pale golden brown on top. The pudding will have a light sponge on top with its own lemon sauce underneath. Serves 4 hungry people or 6 average helpings.

This lemon pudding has something to please everyone, for it combines a hot lemon soufflé with its own built-in sauce.

Chocolate soufflé

4 oz plain chocolate
2 tablespoons water
½ pint milk
1½ oz butter
1½ oz flour
1 teaspoon vanilla essence
4 large eggs
2 oz castor sugar
a little icing sugar

100 gm plain chocolate
2 tablespoons water
300 ml milk
40 gm butter
40 gm flour
1 teaspoon vanilla essence
4 large eggs
50 gm castor sugar
a little icing sugar

Heat the oven to 375°F, 190°C, Gas No. 5 and place a baking sheet in it.

Cut the chocolate into small pieces, put in a pan with the water and 2 tablespoons milk. Stir over a low heat until the chocolate has melted. Add the remaining milk, bring to the boil and remove from the heat.

Melt the butter in a small pan, stir in the flour and cook for 2 minutes without browning. Remove from the heat and stir in the hot milk, return to the heat and bring to the boil, stirring until thickened. Add the vanilla essence and leave to cool.

Separate the eggs and beat the yolks one at a time into the chocolate sauce. Sprinkle on the sugar. Whisk the egg whites using a rotary hand whisk or an electric whisk until stiff but not dry. Stir one tablespoonful into the mixture then carefully fold in the remainder. Pour into a buttered 2 pint (good 1 litre) soufflé dish, run a teaspoon around the edge and bake on the hot baking sheet in the centre of the oven for about 40 minutes. Sprinkle with icing sugar and serve at once with whipped cream. Serves 4.

Variations

Choose any flavouring and add to the mixture before the egg yolks.
Lemon: Add the finely grated rind of 2 small lemons and the juice of ½ a lemon and increase the sugar to 3 oz (75 gm).
Orange: Add the finely grated rind of 2 small oranges and the juice of ½ an orange and increase the sugar to 3 oz (75 gm).
Coffee: Add 2 tablespoons coffee essence to the milk.

So good and not one bit difficult to make as long as you have a rotary whisk or an electric beater to whisk the egg whites. Make sure you use the correct size dish because if you choose a larger one the mixture will not rise above the rim. Serve with whipped cream.

Apple crumble

6 oz plain flour
1½ oz margarine
1½ oz lard
2 oz brown sugar
1½ lb cooking apples
4 oz castor sugar
2 tablespoons water

175 gm plain flour
40 gm margarine
40 gm lard
50 gm brown sugar
675 gm cooking apples
50 gm castor sugar
30 ml water

Heat the oven to 400°F, 200°C, Gas No. 6.

Sift the flour into a bowl and add the fat cut in small pieces. Rub in with the fingertips until the mixture resembles fine breadcrumbs. Stir in the brown sugar.

Peel, core and slice the apples and put in layers into a 1½ pint (1 litre) pie dish with the castor sugar and water. Pile the crumble mixture on top to completely cover the apples and bake in the oven for about 35 minutes until the fruit is cooked and the crumble golden brown. If using cooked apple bake for 30 minutes. Serves 3 to 4.

If you like the flavour of cinnamon add ¼ teaspoon to the crumble mix.

Hot rhubarb and orange

2 lb rhubarb
8 oz granulated sugar
2 rounded tablespoons
    orange marmalade
¼ pint boiling water

900 gm rhubarb
225 gm granulated sugar
2 rounded tablespoons
    orange marmalade
150 ml boiling water

Heat the oven to 325°F, 160°C, Gas No. 3.

Wash the rhubarb and cut into neat 1 inch (2.5 cm) lengths and place in an ovenproof dish with the sugar, marmalade and water. Cover and cook in the oven for ¾ to 1 hour. The time will vary with the age and thickness of the rhubarb, which should be quite tender but still have kept a perfect shape.

If preferred, the rhubarb may be cooked in a slow cooker, in which case it will require 4 to 5 hours on low. Serves 6.

COOK'S TIP

Rhubarb and orange flavours go very well together, and this tastes equally good hot or cold. Serve with lightly whipped cream.

Best bread and butter pudding

6 to 8 slices thin bread, well
    buttered and crusts removed
4 oz dried fruit
grated rind of 1 lemon
2 oz brown sugar
½ pint milk
1 egg

6 to 8 slices thin bread, well
    buttered and crusts removed
100 gm dried fruit
grated rind of 1 lemon
50 gm brown sugar
300 ml milk
1 egg

Butter really well a shallow 1½ pint (1 litre) pie dish. Cut each slice of bread into 3 and arrange half the bread, butter side down, in the dish. Cover with most of the fruit, lemon rind, half the sugar and then top with the remaining bread and butter, butter side uppermost. Sprinkle with the rest of the fruit, lemon rind and sugar.

Blend the milk and egg and strain over the pudding. Leave to soak for at least half an hour, but it is really best to leave it for about 2 hours.

Bake at 350°F, 180°C, Gas No. 4 for 40 minutes or until puffy, pale golden brown and set firm. serve at once. Serves 4.

COOK'S TIP

So good that my children will even go to the fridge and eat it cold if there has been any left! I know that it serves 4 but I must admit that I double up on the amount for my family if it follows a light first course. Use orange instead of lemon if desired.

Cold desserts

Almond cheesecake

4 oz cream cheese, at room
    temperature
4 oz butter, softened
4 oz castor sugar
4 oz semolina
4 eggs, separated
rind and juice of 1 lemon
¾ oz plain flour
1 teaspoon almond essence
¾ oz flaked almonds

**100 gm cream cheese, at room
    temperature
100 gm butter, softened
100 gm castor sugar
100 gm semolina
4 eggs, separated
rind and juice of 1 lemon
18 gm plain flour
5 ml almond essence
18 gm flaked almonds**

Heat the oven to 400°F, 200°C,
Gas No. 6. Grease and line with
greased greaseproof paper an 8
inch (20 cm) round cake tin.

Combine the cream cheese, butter, sugar, semolina, egg yolks,
lemon rind and juice, flour and
almond essence and mix well
together.

Whisk the egg whites with a
hand rotary or electric whisk until
stiff and fold into the mixture.
Turn into the tin and bake in the
oven for 30 minutes. Remove from
the oven and scatter with the flaked
almonds, reduce the oven to
350°F, 180°C, Gas No. 4 and bake
the cheesecake for a further 30
minutes, until firm to the touch
and shrinking away from sides of
tin.

Turn out and remove the paper,
serve hot with the apricot sauce.
Serves 6.

**Serve this cheesecake hot with an
apricot sauce made from warmed
apricot jam thinned down with a
little water and a dash of apricot
brandy if you are feeling flush.**

Grapefruit cheesecake

½ oz gelatine
¼ pint cold water
6 fl oz can concentrated frozen
    grapefruit juice
12 oz rich cream cheese
4 oz castor sugar
¼ pint double cream, whipped

Biscuit topping:
2 oz ginger biscuits, crushed
2 oz digestive biscuits, crushed
1 oz demerara sugar
2 oz butter, melted
fresh grapefruit segments to
    decorate

**15 gm gelatine
150 ml water
175 gm can concentrated frozen
    grapefruit juice
350 gm rich cream cheese
100 gm castor sugar
150 ml double cream, whipped**

Biscuit topping:
**50 gm ginger biscuits, crushed
50 gm digestive biscuits, crushed
25 gm demerara sugar
50 gm butter, melted
fresh grapefruit segments to
    decorate**

Soak the gelatine in cold water for
about 5 minutes, then stand the
bowl in a pan of simmering water

and leave until the gelatine has
dissolved and become quite clear.
Remove from the heat, add the
grapefruit juice and leave to
become cold and nearly set.

Mix the cream cheese with the
sugar and a little of the thick but
not set grapefruit juice. Beat well
and add the rest of the grapefruit
juice mixing well. Lastly fold in the
whipped cream.

Turn into an 8 inch (20 cm) cake
tin with the base lightly greased
then lined with a circle of greaseproof paper. Chill in the refrigerator until set. Mix together the
crushed biscuits, demerara sugar
and butter. Spread over the
cheesecake and chill for a further
hour.

Dip the tin in very hot water for
a moment to loosen the set cheesecake then turn out and decorate
with fresh grapefruit segments.
Serves 6 to 8.

**If liked this cheesecake may be frozen.
Open freeze until solid without crust,
overwrap and return to the freezer,
use within 3 months. Leave to thaw
overnight in the refrigerator, then
put on the crust, chill for 1 hour then
turn out and decorate with grapefruit
segments.
You can also use tinned juice, but it is
not as nice. A green kiwi fruit (it used
to be called Chinese gooseberry) sliced
makes a different, more special
decoration for a party.
Don't make this in a loose-
bottomed cake tin, as the cheesecake
mixture could seep out before it has
set. The cheesecake is poured into the
cake tin and left to set. Then the
biscuit crust is put on top, so when
you reverse the cheesecake out of the
tin the biscuit crust is underneath.**

Apple jelly with grapes

1 packet lime jelly
¼ pint boiling water
½ pint apple juice
8 oz large green grapes

1 packet lime jelly
150 ml boiling water
300 ml apple juice
225 gm large green grapes

Dissolve the jelly in the boiling water. Stir in the apple juice.

Halve the grapes and remove all the pips.

Pour ⅓ of the liquid into the jelly mould and stir in the grapes. Leave to set in the refrigerator, then pour in the remaining jelly. Should this have started to set, heat it slightly so that it melts before pouring it into the mould. Leave until set and thoroughly chill before turning out and serving. Serves 4.

To turn out a jelly, first dip the mould quickly into very hot water. Put a plate on top of it and turn sharply upside down. If you have previously wetted the plate you will be able to slide the jelly into a central position should it not land in the middle of the plate.

Black forest cheesecake

6 digestive biscuits, crushed
1½ oz butter, melted
3 eggs, separated
4 oz castor sugar
1 lb cream cheese at room temperature
½ teaspoon vanilla essence
15 oz can black cherries, preferably stoned
1 rounded teaspoon arrowroot

6 digestive biscuits, crushed
40 gm butter, melted
3 eggs, separated
100 gm castor sugar
450 gm cream cheese at room temperature
2.5 ml vanilla essence
425 gm can black cherries, preferably stoned
1 rounded teaspoon arrowroot

Heat the oven to 350°F, 180°C, Gas No. 4. Lightly butter and flour a 7 inch (17.5 cm) round loose-bottomed cake tin.

Blend the biscuits with the melted butter and press firmly over the base of the cake tin.

Whisk the egg yolks and sugar until light and creamy and stir in the cream cheese and vanilla essence until well blended. Whisk the egg whites using a hand, rotary or electric whisk until stiff, fold into the cheese mixture and spoon into the tin. Bake in the oven for about 1½ hours, until well risen and pale golden brown and shrinking slightly away from the sides of the tin, then turn off the heat and leave in the oven for a further 15 to 30 minutes. Remove from the oven and leave to cool in the tin until quite cold. Then remove the cake from the tin and place on a serving dish.

Drain the cherries and, if necessary, stone. Reserve the juice and blend ¼ pint (150 ml) with the arrowroot in a small saucepan and then slowly bring to the boil, stirring until thickened. Add the cherries and mix lightly. Spoon over the cheesecake and leave to cool completely. Chill before serving. Serves 6 to 8.

Black Forest cheesecake is cooked, so expect it to sink slightly in the centre on cooling. For an extra special occasion, fill the dip with cherries in a sauce, laced with a couple of tablespoons (30 ml) kirsch.

Chocolate meringue gâteau

3 egg whites
6 oz castor sugar

Chocolate filling:
¼ pint milk
2 oz castor sugar
2 oz plain chocolate
3 egg yolks
1 level teaspoon cornflour
6 oz unsalted butter, softened

Topping:
¼ pint double cream, whipped
12 Maltesers

3 egg whites
175 gm castor sugar

Chocolate filling:
150 ml milk
50 gm castor sugar
50 gm plain chocolate
3 egg yolks
1 level teaspoon cornflour
175 gm unsalted butter, softened

Topping:
150 ml double cream, whipped
12 Maltesers

Heat the oven to 300°F, 150°C, Gas No. 2 and line 2 large baking sheets with non-stick silicone paper.

Meringue: put the egg whites in a large bowl and whisk with a hand rotary or an electric whisk until stiff. Gradually whisk in the sugar a teaspoonful at a time. Spread the meringue in 2 circles 8 inches (20 cm) in diameter on the baking sheets and bake for 1 hour in the oven, then turn off the heat and leave in the oven to cool.

Chocolate filling: first make the chocolate custard sauce. Put the milk, sugar and chocolate broken into small pieces in a basin and place over a pan of hot water. Heat gently until the chocolate has melted and blended with the milk. Stir a little of the hot liquid onto the egg yolks, blend with the cornflour and then add to the remaining chocolate mixture and stir until thickened. This will take about 5 to 10 minutes and is ready when the sauce will coat the back of the spoon. Remove from the heat and leave to become quite cold.

Cream the butter and beat in the chocolate sauce. If by any chance the butter cream should curdle because the butter and chocolate custard are not at the same temperature, warm the bowl slightly by standing in hot water and then beat well.

Spread half the chocolate cream on one meringue layer then cover with the other meringue. Spread the remaining chocolate cream over this and mark attractively with a palette knife.

Topping: pipe the double cream in 12 large rosettes around the edge or over the top of the gâteau and press a Malteser into the centre of each rosette. Keep in the refrigerator until required and then allow to stand at room temperature for 2 to 3 hours before serving. Serves 6.

This is an impressive looking meringue gâteau which can be made the day before it is needed as it improves with keeping for a day.

Chocolate and orange mousse

½ oz gelatine
1 tablespoon water
rind and juice of 1 orange
8 oz plain chocolate
5 eggs, separated
4 oz castor sugar
½ pint whipping cream, whipped

12.5 gm gelatine
1 tablespoon water
rind and juice of 1 orange
225 gm plain chocolate
5 eggs, separated
100 gm castor sugar
300 ml whipping cream, whipped

Soak the gelatine in the water with the rind and juice of the orange in a small cup or basin and leave until it becomes spongy. Then stand in a pan of simmering water until it has completely dissolved and is runny.

Put another basin containing the chocolate broken into small pieces over the pan of hot water and leave until melted. Add the 5 egg yolks and stir until smooth.

Pour the gelatine into a small mixing bowl and stir in the chocolate mixture and leave for 5 minutes until cool but not set.

Meanwhile whisk the egg whites using a hand electric or rotary whisk until frothy then add the sugar a teaspoonful at a time whisking all the time until you have the consistency of a meringue. Quickly fold in the chocolate, yolk, orange and gelatine mixture then fold in half the whipped cream. Turn into individual glass dishes, cover with cling film and chill until set. Then decorate with chocolate and swirls of the remaining whipped cream. Serves 6 to 8.

This is sinfully rich and takes time to make but it is well worth it for a special occasion.

Rosy red fruit salad

1 large orange
4 cloves
1 lb blackcurrants
½ lb blackberries
6 oz granulated sugar
¼ pint water
8 oz raspberries
1 lb fresh pears, peeled, cored and sliced

1 large orange
4 cloves
450 gm blackcurrants
225 gm blackberries
175 gm granulated sugar
150 ml water
225 gm raspberries
450 gm fresh pears, peeled, cored and sliced

This uses mostly frozen fruit and is especially good served with lightly whipped cream or ice cream.

Cut strips of peel from the orange, stick in the cloves and place in a saucepan with the blackcurrants, blackberries, sugar and water, cover and simmer gently for 10 minutes or until tender.

Turn into a bowl, remove and discard the orange peel, cut the orange into segments. Leave to cool, then chill thoroughly.

Stir in the raspberries, pears and orange just before serving. Serves 6.

Melon mint sorbet

scant ¾ pint water
6 oz castor sugar
rind and juice of 2 lemons
2 egg whites, lightly whipped
half an Ogen or Galia melon
leaves of 6 young sprigs of mint

scant 450 ml water
175 gm castor sugar
rind and juice of 2 lemons
2 egg whites, lightly whipped
half an Ogen or Galia melon
leaves of 6 young sprigs of mint

Put the water and sugar in a saucepan and stir over low heat until the sugar has dissolved. Add the thinly pared rind of the lemons; use a vegetable peeler and pare off only the fine outer yellow zest. Bring to the boil and then boil rapidly for 5 minutes, draw off the heat, strain into a bowl and leave to cool.

Add the strained lemon juice and lightly whipped egg whites. Remove the seeds from the melon and scoop out the fruit from the skin. Place the melon in a blender with the mint leaves and puree until smooth. Stir into the lemon mixture, pour into a rigid plastic container, cover and freeze for about 3 hours until the mixture is mushy.

Spoon the partially frozen mixture into a large bowl and whisk until smooth and white.

Return the mixture to the container, cover, label and freeze. Put the melon shell in a plastic bag and freeze too. When required, serve the sorbet in scoops in the melon shell. Serves 8.

A delicious refreshing sweet to serve after a heavy main course.

Lemon ice cream

4 eggs, separated
4 oz castor sugar
½ pint double cream
grated rind and juice of 2 lemons

4 eggs, separated
100 gm castor sugar
300 ml double cream
grated rind and juice of 2 lemons

Whisk the yolks in a small bowl until blended. In a larger bowl whisk the egg whites with a hand rotary or electric whisk until stiff, then whisk in the sugar a teaspoonful at a time.

Whisk the cream with the lemon rind and juice until it forms soft peaks and then fold into the meringue mixture with the egg yolks.

Turn into a 2½ pint (1.4 litre) container, cover, label and freeze.

Leave to thaw at room temperature for 5 minutes then serve in scoops in small glasses or dishes. Serves 6 to 8.

A quick easy ice cream with a sharp lemon flavour. No need to whip the ice cream half way through freezing as it is beautifully creamy without.

Praline ice cream

1½ oz whole blanched almonds
5½ oz castor sugar
4 eggs
½ pint whipping cream

40 gm whole blanched almonds
162.5 gm castor sugar
4 eggs
300 ml whipping cream

Put the almonds with 1½ oz (40 gm) castor sugar in a heavy pan and place over a low heat, stirring occasionally until the sugar has melted and is beginning to caramelize.

This will take about 15 minutes. Continue to cook until the mixture is an even golden brown and the nuts are glazed. Remove from the heat and pour onto an oiled enamel plate or baking tray. Leave until quite firm and cold. Turn into a grinder or blender and grind coarsely or crush with a rolling pin.

Separate the eggs, place the yolks in a small bowl and whisk until well blended. In another larger bowl whisk the egg whites until stiff and then whisk in the remaining castor sugar a spoonful at a time. Whisk the cream until it forms soft peaks and fold into the meringue mixture with the egg yolks and praline.

Turn into a 2½ pint (1.5 litre) rigid container, cover, label and freeze.

Remove from the refrigerator and leave to stand for 5 minutes. Serve in scoops in individual glasses with brandy snaps. Serves 6 to 8.

Place the breadcrumbs and soft brown sugar on an enamel or foil plate and toast under a hot grill until golden brown and caramelized, stirring occasionally. Keep a sharp eye whilst the crumbs are browning, and wait for them to turn a dark horsechestnut colour. This will take 5 to 8 minutes. Leave to become quite cold.

Whisk the egg yolks in a small bowl until well blended. In another bowl whisk the egg whites with a hand rotary whisk or an electric whisk until stiff, then whisk in the castor sugar, a teaspoonful at a time. Whisk the cream until it forms soft peaks, then fold into the egg-white mixture with the yolks and breadcrumbs.

Turn into a 2½ pint (1.5 litre) container, cover, label and freeze.

Leave to thaw at room temperature for 5 minutes, then serve in scoops in glass dishes. Serves 6 to 8.

FROM LEFT TO RIGHT: *A delicious refreshing Melon mint sorbet, a rich Lemon ice cream, a crunchy Praline ice cream.*

This ice cream is delicious served with brandy snaps because of the unexpected crunchy pieces of caramel it contains.

Caramel ice cream

3 oz fresh brown breadcrumbs
3 oz soft brown sugar
4 eggs, separated
2 oz castor sugar
½ pint double cream

75 gm fresh brown breadcrumbs
75 gm soft brown sugar
4 eggs, separated
50 gm castor sugar
300 ml double cream

Brown bread in ice cream: very unusual, but well worth trying. The brown crumbs are caramelized with sugar until crisp and crunchy, then folded into home-made ice cream.

41

Blackberry mousse

1 lb blackberries
4 oz castor sugar
juice of 1 small lemon
3 tablespoons cold water
½ oz gelatine
¼ pint double cream
2 egg whites

450 gm blackberries
100 gm castor sugar
juice of 1 small lemon
3 tablespoons cold water
12.5 gm gelatine
150 ml double cream
2 egg whites

Wash and pick over the blackberries and put in a saucepan with the sugar and lemon juice. Place over a low heat and simmer gently for about 10 minutes with the lid on until the blackberries are soft and the juice is running out.

Put the water in a small bowl or cup and sprinkle over the gelatine. Soak for 5 minutes.

Take the fruit from the heat and stir in the soaked gelatine until it has dissolved. Sieve the fruit into a large bowl to make a puree and leave on one side until beginning to thicken and quite cold.

Lightly whisk all but one tablespoon of the cream and whisk the egg whites with a hand or electric whisk until stiff. Fold the whisked cream and egg whites into the puree until blended and turn into a 2 pint (1 litre) glass serving dish. Swirl the last spoonful of cream into the centre of the mousse and leave in a cool place until set. Serves 6.

Blackberries will give a superb strong flavour to mousses and team deliciously with apples in pies or crumbles. The best thing about them is that they are free.

Pavlova

3 egg whites
6 oz castor sugar
1 teaspoon vinegar
1 level teaspoon cornflour
½ pint whipped whipping cream
8 oz frozen raspberries,
    just thawed
a little castor sugar to sweeten

3 egg whites
175 gm castor sugar
1 teaspoon vinegar
1 level teaspoon cornflour
300 ml whipped whipping cream
225 gm frozen rasepberries,
    just thawed
a little castor sugar to sweeten

Lay a sheet of silicone paper (non-stick vegetable parchment) on a baking tray and mark an 8 inch (20 cm) circle on it. Heat the oven to 325°F, 160°C, Gas No. 3.

Whisk the egg whites with a hand rotary or electric whisk until stiff, then whisk in the sugar a spoonful at a time. Blend the vinegar with the cornflour and whisk into the egg whites with the last spoonful of sugar.

Spread the meringue out to cover the circle on the baking tray, building up the sides so that they are higher than the centre.

Put in the centre of the oven, turn the heat down to 300°F, 150°C, Gas No. 2 and bake for 1 hour. The pavlova will be a pale creamy colour rather than white. Turn the oven off and leave the pavlova to become quite cold in the oven.

Remove from the baking tray and place on a serving dish.

Fold the cream and raspberries together lightly and sweeten to

taste. Pile into the centre of the pavlova and leave to stand for an hour in the refrigerator before serving. Serves 6.

This is very like meringue but the middle is lovely and soft.

Thomas's flan

Flan case:
2 oz butter or margarine
1 level tablespoon sugar
8 digestive biscuits, crushed

Filling:
6 oz can condensed milk
¼ pint double cream
juice of 2 lemons
halved grapes to decorate

Flan case:
50 gm butter or margarine
1 level tablespoon sugar
8 digestive biscuits, crushed

Filling:
175 gm can condensed milk
150 ml double cream
juice of 2 lemons
halved grapes to decorate

Melt the butter or margarine in a saucepan, remove from the heat and stir in the sugar and crushed biscuits. Mix well and press the mixture over the base and sides of a 7 inch (17.5 cm) flan ring or loose-bottomed flan tin. Spread evenly using a metal tablespoon.

Put the condensed milk, cream and lemon juice in a bowl and whisk the mixture together until well blended. Pour into the flan case.

Chill for at least 4 hours in the refrigerator. Before serving remove the flan ring and decorate with halved grapes. Serves 4-6.

This is a flan so easy to make that it is ideal for children's cooking.

Apricot and almond tart

Shortcrust pastry:
6 oz plain flour
1½ oz margarine
1½ oz lard
about 6 teaspoons cold water

Filling:
4 oz butter
4 oz castor sugar
1 egg, beaten
4 oz ground rice or semolina
½ teaspoon almond essence
1 heaped tablespoon apricot jam

Shortcrust pastry:
175 gm plain flour
40 gm margarine
40 gm lard
about 30 ml cold water

Filling:
100 gm butter
100 gm castor sugar
1 egg, beaten
100 gm ground rice or semolina
2.5 ml almond essence
1 heaped tablespoon apricot jam

Heat the oven to 400°F, 200°C, Gas No. 6.

Make the pastry in the usual way and roll out thinly on a floured table. Line an 8 inch (20 cm) fluted flan ring which should be placed on a baking tray. Prick the base of the flan with a fork and leave in the refrigerator for 10 minutes.

Prepare the filling: heat the butter in a small pan until it has melted but is not brown. Stir in the sugar and cook for one minute, then stir in the egg, ground rice and almond essence. Spread the jam over the base of the flan and pour over the filling. Roll out the pastry trimmings and cut them into strips ½ inch (1.25 cm) wide and arrange them in a lattice on top of the pudding, making them stick with a little milk.

Bake in the oven for about 30 minutes or until well risen and golden brown. The filling should then spring back into shape when lightly pressed with a finger. Take the tart out of the oven, remove the flan ring and leave to cool on a wire rack. If liked, spoon a little apricot jam, laced with liqueur for special occasions, in alternate squares of lattice. Serves 4 to 6.

You would never guess that this tart actually contains no almonds. It tastes very almondy and is best served warm.

Chocolate Juliette

8 oz milk chocolate
8 oz margarine
2 eggs
1 oz castor sugar
8 oz 'Nice' biscuits
¼ pint double cream, whipped
chocolate buttons or matchsticks

225 gm milk chocolate
225 gm margarine
2 eggs
25 gm castor sugar
225 gm 'Nice' biscuits
150 ml double cream, whipped
chocolate buttons or matchsticks

Line a small loaf tin 7½ inches (19 cm) by 4 inches (10 cm) by 2½ inches (6 cm) with foil.

Break the chocolate into small pieces and place in a pan with the margarine and heat gently until melted. Beat the eggs and sugar together until blended, then gradually add the chocolate mixture a little at a time. Break the biscuits into ½ inch (1.5 cm) pieces and stir into the chocolate mixture. Pack into the tin and smooth the top. Leave to set in the refrigerator for about 6 hours or until firm.

Turn out onto a serving dish and peel off the foil. Cover with the cream and decorate with chocolate buttons or chocolate matchsticks. Serves 8 to 10.

A very rich confection, so serve in thin slices — they can always come back for more.

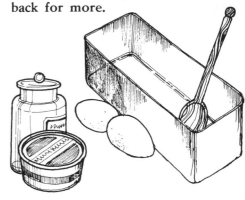

Quick lemon cheesecake

¼ pint boiling water
1 lemon jelly
juice of 2 lemons and the rind of 1 lemon
12 oz rich cream cheese
¼ pint double cream
3 to 4 oz castor sugar
2 oz digestive biscuits, crushed
2 oz ginger biscuits, crushed
1 oz demerara sugar
2 oz butter, melted
a little soured cream
lemon slices

150 ml boiling water
1 lemon jelly
juice of 2 lemons and the rind of 1 lemon
350 gm rich cream cheese
150 ml double cream
75 to 100 gm castor sugar
50 gm digestive biscuits, crushed
50 gm ginger biscuits, crushed
25 gm demerara sugar
50 gm butter, melted
a little soured cream
lemon slices

Put the boiling water in a measuring jug with the jelly and stir until dissolved. Add the lemon rind and juice and if necessary make up to ½ pint (300 ml) with extra cold water. Leave to become quite cold and nearly set.

Mix the cream cheese with a little of the cream and whisk the remainder until it forms soft peaks; fold into cheese with castor sugar and almost-set jelly mixture. Turn into an 8 inch (20 cm) cake tin lined with a circle of greaseproof paper and chill in the refrigerator until set.

Mix together the crushed biscuits, sugar and melted butter and spread over the cheesecake; chill for a further hour.

Dip tin into very hot water for a brief moment to loosen cheesecake, then turn out onto a serving dish, remove the circle of greaseproof paper and spread the top with soured cream. Before serving decorate with lemon slices.

The crust of this cheesecake needs explaining: it is put on top of the cheesecake when in the cake tin so that when you reverse the tin to turn it out onto a flat plate the crust is underneath.

eggs, sugar and vanilla essence. Warm milk in a saucepan over low heat until it is hand-hot, then pour it onto egg mixture, stirring constantly.

Butter the sides of the mould or tin above the caramel. Strain the crème into the mould or tin and place in a roasting tin half-filled with hot water. Bake in an oven preheated to 300°F, 150°C, Gas No. 2, for 1½ hours or until a knife inserted into the centre of it comes out clean. Don't worry if it takes longer to cook than the time given; it will set eventually. Don't increase oven temperature or the crème will have bubbles in.

Remove it from the oven and leave to cool completely for at least 12 hours or overnight. Turn out carefully on to a flat serving dish. Serves 4.

Next day, whip the remaining cream and use it to completely cover the roll. Decorate with slices of stem ginger or whole fresh strawberries. To serve, cut the roll in diagonal slices. Serves 4 to 6.

A first-class, easy pudding, which you can prepare the day before then decorate the next day.

Strawberry brûlée

1 lb strawberries, sliced
3 oz castor sugar
juice and rind of 1 orange
a little orange liqueur (optional)
¼ pint double cream, whipped
¼ pint plain yoghurt
3 oz demerara sugar

450 gm strawberries, sliced
75 gm castor sugar
juice and rind of 1 orange
a little orange liqueur (optional)
150 ml double cream, whipped
150 ml plain yoghurt
75 gm demerara sugar

Lay the strawberries in a shallow 1½ pint (1 litre) heatproof dish and sprinkle with the castor sugar, orange juice and rind and liqueur if used.

Mix the double cream and yoghurt and spread over the fruit. Chill in the refrigerator for at least 6 hours until thoroughly cold.

Sprinkle with demerara sugar and brown under a hot grill for 4 to 5 minutes until the sugar has melted and become crisp. Serve at once. Serves 4.

Such a simple pudding and very special. You can if you wish use canned white peaches or fresh seeded large grapes instead of strawberries.

Crème caramel

Caramel:
3 oz granulated sugar
3 tablespoons water

Crème:
4 eggs
1½ oz castor sugar
few drops vanilla essence
1 pint milk

Caramel:
75 gm granulated sugar
3 tablespoons water

Crème:
4 eggs
50 gm castor sugar
few drops vanilla essence
600 ml milk

To make caramel: put the sugar and water in a heavy saucepan and dissolve sugar over low heat. Bring to the boil and boil until syrup is pale golden brown. Remove from the heat and quickly pour caramel syrup into the bottom of a 1½ pint (1 litre) charlotte mould or cake tin.

For the crème: mix together

Never turn out the caramel custard until the moment of serving as it loses its gloss and colour with standing when turned out.

Brandy ginger roll

½ pint whipping cream
8 oz ginger biscuits
4 tablespoons brandy
slices of stem ginger or fresh
    strawberries to decorate

300 ml whipping cream
225 gm ginger biscuits
60 ml brandy
slices of stem ginger or fresh
    strawberries to decorate

Put half the cream in a bowl and whisk with a rotary or electric whisk until it forms fairly stiff peaks. Quickly dip each biscuit in a little brandy and then sandwich together with cream shaping into a long roll, place on a serving dish and leave in a cool place or a refrigerator overnight.

45

Quick lemon mousse

4 eggs
4 oz castor sugar
2 large lemons
½ oz gelatine
3 tablespoons cold water
whipped cream and lemon slices
   to decorate

4 eggs
100 gm castor sugar
2 large lemons
12.5 gm gelatine
3 tablespoons cold water
whipped cream and lemon slices
   to decorate

Separate the eggs, place the yolks
in a bowl with the sugar and beat
until well blended and creamy. Put
the whites in a bowl ready for
whisking.

Grate the rind and squeeze the
juice from the lemons and add
both to the yolk mixture.

Place the gelatine and water in a
small bowl or cup. Leave for 3
minutes until thick, then stand the
bowl in a pan of simmering water
and allow the gelatine to dissolve.
Cool slightly and add to the yolk
and lemon mixture; leave to cool
but not set.

Whisk the egg whites, using a
rotary or electric whisk until stiff,
then fold into the lemon mixture.
Put into a 2 pint (1 litre) glass dish
and chill for at least 4 hours to set.

Decorate with whipped cream
and lemon slices and serve at room
temperature. Serves 6.

A very simple sharp mousse. I find it
popular after a large meal especially at
Christmas time.

Gooseberry fool

1 lb gooseberries
2 tablespoons water
3 to 4 oz castor sugar
17 fl oz family brick vanilla
   ice cream
a little green colouring

450 gm gooseberries
2 tablespoons water
75 to 100 gm castor sugar
510 ml family brick vanilla
   ice cream
a little green colouring

Place the gooseberries in a
saucepan with the water, cover and
cook gently until tender for about
15 to 20 minutes. Remove from the
heat and sieve into a bowl, add
sugar to taste and leave the puree
to become quite cold.

Remove the ice cream from the
freezer and leave to soften at room
temperature for about 10 to 15
minutes. Stir the ice cream into the
puree and mix until well blended.
If liked add a little green colouring.

Turn into a dish and serve with
brandy snaps. Serves 4.

An ideal pudding if you're in a hurry;
being tart and light it is often
welcome after a heavy or rich meal.

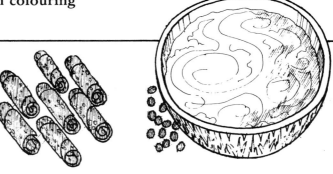

Home baking

Victoria sandwich

4 oz soft margarine or butter
4 oz castor sugar
2 large eggs, beaten
4 oz self-raising flour
4 tablespoons strawberry jam
2 to 3 teaspoons castor sugar

100 gm soft margarine or butter
100 gm castor sugar
2 large eggs, beaten
100 gm self-raising flour
4 tablespoons strawberry jam
2 to 3 teaspoons castor sugar

Heat the oven to 350°F, 180°C, Gas No. 4. Grease and line with greased greasproof paper two 7 inch (17.5 cm) straight-sided sandwich tins.

Cream the margarine and sugar until light and fluffy. Add the egg a little at a time, beating well after each addition. Sieve the flour and add a spoonful with the last amount of egg to prevent it curdling Fold in the remaining flour with a metal spoon to make a soft dropping consistency. Divide the mixture equally between the tins.

Bake in the oven for 25 to 30 minutes. When the cake is cooked the colour should be a pale golden and the centre of the sponge will spring back into place when lightly pressed with the finger.

Turn the sponges onto a wire rack to cool and remove the paper. When completely cold, sandwich together with strawberry jam and sprinkle with castor sugar.

Variations:
Orange: add the finely grated rind of an orange to the creamed mixture.

Chocolate: replace 1 oz (25 gm) of flour with 1 oz (25 gm) cocoa.

Cocoa: dissolve 1 heaped teaspoon instant coffee powder in the beaten eggs before adding to the mixture.

One of the classic British cakes. Do not feel you have to use butter. I now use soft margarine for everyday and I find the results excellent.

Special cherry cake

6 oz glacé cherries
8 oz self-raising flour
6 oz soft margarine
6 oz castor sugar
finely grated rind of 1 lemon
3 eggs
2 oz ground almonds

175 gm glacé cherries
225 gm self-raising flour
175 gm soft margarine
175 gm castor sugar
finely grated rind of 1 lemon
3 eggs
50 gm ground almonds

Heat the oven to 350°F, 180°C, Gas No. 4. Grease and line with greased greaseproof paper a 7 inch (17.5 cm) round cake tin.

Put the cherries in a sieve and rinse under running water, drain well and dry very thoroughly on absorbent kitchen paper, then cut each cherry in quarters.

Place all the remaining ingredients except the cherries in a bowl and beat well for 1 minute and then lightly fold in the cherries. The mixture will be of a fairly stiff dropping consistency which will help keep the cherries evenly suspended in the cake while it is baking.

Turn the mixture into the tin and bake in the oven for about 1 hour 20 minutes or until a skewer inserted in the centre of the cake comes out clean. Leave to cool in the tin for 5 minutes, then turn out onto a wire rack to finish cooling; remove the paper and when quite cold wrap in foil or store in an airtight tin.

It is important to wash any sugar off the cherries and to dry them.

Special apple dessert cake

5 oz butter
2 large eggs
8 oz castor sugar
1 teaspoon almond essence
8 oz self-raising flour
1 ½ level teaspoons baking powder
1 ½ lb cooking apples, before
   peeling
icing sugar

150 gm butter
2 large eggs
225 gm castor sugar
5 ml almond essence
225 gm self-raising flour
1.5 level teaspoons baking
   powder
675 gm cooking apples, before
   peeling
icing sugar

Heat the oven to 375°F, 190°C, Gas No. 5. Grease well a 10 inch (25 cm) loose-bottomed cake tin.

Melt the butter in a pan over a medium heat until just runny and pour into a large bowl. Add the eggs, sugar and almond essence and beat well until mixed. Fold in the flour and baking powder. Spread just under two thirds of the mixture in the cake tin. Then straight away peel, core and slice the apples and arrange roughly on top of the mixture. Spread the remaining mixture over the apples. It is difficult to get this last bit of mixture smooth, but don't worry as the blobs even out during cooking.

Bake for 1½ hours, until the apple is tender when prodded with a skewer. Loosen the sides of the cake with a knife and carefully push the cake out.

Dust over very generously with icing sugar when slightly cooled and serve warm or cold with lots of lightly whipped or thick cream.

Keep covered in the fridge and eat within 4 days. Serves about 12.

TOP TO BOTTOM: *Special dessert cake, Marmalade fruitcake, Mincemeat cake*

This is highly delicious and very quick to make. You can serve it as a cake or a pudding.

Tacky gingerbread

1 level teaspoon mixed spice
1 level teaspoon bicarbonate
  of soda
2 level teaspoons ground ginger
8 oz plain flour
3 oz lard
4 oz black treacle
4 oz golden syrup
2 oz soft brown sugar
2 oz chunky marmalade,
  roughly chopped
2 eggs, beaten
6 tablespoons milk
2 oz sultanas
2 oz chopped stem ginger, optional

1 level teaspoon mixed spice
1 level teaspoon bicarbonate
  of soda
2 level teaspoons ground ginger
225 gm plain flour
75 gm lard
100 gm black treacle
100 gm golden syrup
50 gm chunky marmalade,
  roughly chopped
2 eggs, beaten
90 ml milk
50 gm sultanas
50 gm chopped stem ginger,
  optional

Grease and line with greased greaseproof paper an 8 inch (20 cm) square tin or a 7½ by 9½ inch (19 by 24.5 cm) meat roasting tin. Heat the oven to 325°F, 160°C, Gas No. 3.

Sift spices, bicarbonate of soda and flour into a large mixing bowl and make a well in the centre.

Place the lard in a saucepan with the treacle, syrup and sugar and heat until the lard has just melted and the ingredients blended, draw from the heat and cool slightly. Stir the marmalade, eggs, milk, sultanas and stem ginger into the bowl of flour with the lard mixture and beat with a wooden spoon until smooth and glossy.

Pour into the tin and bake in the oven for 1 to 1¼ hours. Leave to cool in the tin for about 30 minutes, then turn out and remove the paper and finish cooling on a wire rack. Store in an airtight tin until required.

Gingerbread tastes even better if it is kept for 2 to 3 days before cutting.

Marmalade fruitcake

6 oz soft margarine
6 oz soft brown sugar
12 oz mixed dried fruit
3 large eggs, beaten
9 oz self-raising flour
2 oz glacé cherries, quartered
2 level tablespoons chopped
  chunky marmalade

175 gm soft margarine
175 gm soft brown sugar
350 gm mixed dried fruit
3 large eggs, beaten
250 gm self-raising flour
50 gm glacé cherries, quartered
2 level tablespoons chopped
  chunky marmalade

Heat the oven to 325°F, 160°C, Gas No. 3. Grease and line an 8 inch (20 cm) round cake tin with greased greaseproof paper.

Put all the ingredients together in a bowl and mix well until blended. Turn into the tin and spread evenly leaving a slight hollow in the top. Bake just above the centre of the oven for about 2¼ hours; when the cake is pierced with a skewer in the centre it will come out clean. Leave to cool in the tin for 10 minutes, then turn out onto a wire rack and leave until cold.

A first-rate family fruit cake, but don't overdo the marmalade otherwise the fruit will sink to the bottom.

Mincemeat cake

5 oz soft margarine
5 oz castor sugar
2 eggs
8 oz self-raising flour
3 oz currants
1 lb jar mincemeat
1 oz flaked almonds

150 gm soft margarine
150 gm castor sugar
2 eggs
225 gm self-raising flour
75 gm currants
450 gm jar mincemeat
25 gm flaked almonds

Grease and line with greased greaseproof paper an 8 inch (20 cm) round cake tin. Heat the oven to 325°F, 160°C, Gas No. 3.

Place all the ingredients except the almonds together in a bowl and beat for one minute until blended. Turn into the tin and smooth the top. Arrange the almonds on the top and bake in the oven for about 1¾ hours until golden brown and shrinking away from the sides of the tin. Leave to cool in the tin and then remove the paper and store in an airtight container.

As you would expect, this cake is very moist, lightly fruited and, frankly, absolutely delicious. It is a newly invented recipe of mine that I dare not make too often as I enjoy it so much and it is by no means slimming.

Yum yums

8 oz soft margarine
6 oz castor sugar
1 egg, beaten
10 oz self-raising flour
2 oz cornflakes, lightly crushed

225 gm soft margarine
175 gm castor sugar
1 egg, beaten
275 gm self-raising flour
50 gm cornflakes, lightly crushed

Heat the oven to 375°F, 190°C, Gas No. 5 and grease 3 large baking sheets.

Put the margarine into a large bowl, add sugar and cream together with a wooden spoon until soft. Beat in the egg, then slowly work in the flour until the mixture has come together. If it is a warm day or the kitchen is hot the mixture may be rather soft to handle, so wrap it in cling film and chill for 10 minutes.

Wet the hands and lightly roll mixture into about 34 balls and roll each one in the crushed cornflakes. Position well spaced on the baking sheets and slightly flatten each with the hand. Bake for about 20 to 25 minutes until turning a very pale brown at the edges. Remove from the oven and leave on the trays for 1 minute before carefully lifting each biscuit onto a wire rack to cool. When quite cold store in an airtight tin. Makes about 34.

These are really good home-made biscuits and ideal for children to make from ingredients that you have in the store cupboard.

Scottish shortbread

6 oz plain flour
3 oz cornflour
6 oz butter
3 oz castor sugar

175 gm plain flour
75 gm cornflour
175 gm butter
75 gm castor sugar

Heat the oven to 325°F, 160°C, Gas No. 3.

Sift the flour and cornflour together. Cream the butter until soft. Add the sugar and beat until light and fluffy. Work in the flours then knead well together.

Press out the shortbread into a shallow greased baking tin 11 inches by 7 (28 cm by 17.5) flattening the dough with knuckles. Prick well with a fork and mark into 16 fingers with the back of a knife.

Chill in the refrigerator for 15 minutes, then bake in the oven for about 35 minutes or until a very pale golden brown. Leave to cool in the tin for 15 minutes then cut through where the shortbread is marked and then carefully lift onto a wire rack to finish cooling. Makes 16 pieces.

Butter is an absolute must for shortbread because the flavour really does come through. A proportion of cornflour, semolina and ground rice adds a crispy texture. Keep in an airtight tin.

Crunchjacks

5 oz soft margarine
5 oz demerara sugar
5 oz quick porridge oats
1 oz desiccated coconut

150 gm soft margarine
150 gm demerara sugar
150 gm quick porridge oats
25 gm desiccated coconut

Heat the oven to 325°F, 160°C, Gas No. 3 and grease a shallow baking tin 11 inches by 7 (28 cm by 17.5).

Cream the margarine and sugar together until well blended and

then stir in the oats and coconut and mix thoroughly.

Press into the tin and bake for 40 to 45 minutes until golden brown. Remove from the oven and leave for 10 minutes, then mark into 18 squares and leave to become quite cold in the tin.

Lift out of the tin and store in an airtight container. Makes 18 Crunch jacks.

Emma's biscuits

4 oz margarine
1 rounded tablespoon golden
  syrup
5 oz (1 level carton) castor sugar
3 oz (1½ cartons) rolled oats
2½ oz (1 level carton) self-raising
  flour

100 gm margarine
1 rounded tablespoon golden
  syrup
150 gm castor sugar
75 gm rolled oats
65 gm self-raising flour

This is an ideal recipe for children, and to make it easier for them they can use an empty 5 oz (150 ml) yoghurt or cream carton to measure out the ingredients.

Heat the oven to 325°F, 160°C, Gas No. 3 and grease two large baking trays.

Put the margarine, syrup and sugar in a saucepan and place over a low heat until the margarine has just melted. Remove from the heat and stir in the oats and flour, mix well.

Allow the mixture to cool slightly, then roll into small balls and place well spaced on the baking trays. Bake for about 20 minutes until a pale golden brown all over. Remove from the oven and leave for a few minutes before placing on a wire rack to cool. Store in an airtight tin. Makes 30 biscuits.

FROM LEFT TO RIGHT: *Yum yums, Scottish shortbread, Crunchjacks*

When you are asked for goodies for a coffee morning or bazaar you can be sure that these will always go down well. They seem to be popular with all ages and never stay in the biscuit tin for long. To my mind they are rather nicer than flapjacks.

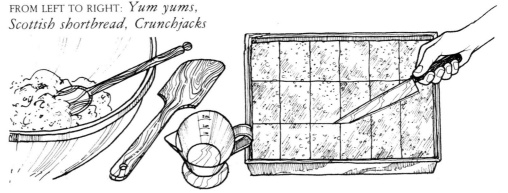

Strawberry shortbread

4 ½ oz plain flour
3 oz butter
1 ½ oz castor sugar
¾ lb strawberries
3 tablespoons redcurrant jelly
a little whipped cream

125 gm plain flour
75 gm butter
40 gm castor sugar
350 gm strawberries
3 tablespoons redcurrant jelly
a little whipped cream

Sift the flour into a bowl, add the butter and sugar and rub in the butter until the mixture resembles fine breadcrumbs, knead together then turn on to a table and knead lightly for 3 minutes until the mixture is smooth. Roll or pat out the shortbread on a baking sheet to a round ¼ inch (½ cm) thick and 8 inches (20 cm) in diameter, crimp the edges and leave to chill in the refrigerator for 20 minutes.

Heat the oven to 325°F, 170°C, Gas No. 3 and bake the shortbread for 25 to 30 minutes until a pale golden brown. Leave to cool on the baking sheet.

When quite cold transfer to a serving dish. Hull the strawberries, cut in half and arrange on the shortbread. Heat the redcurrant jelly in a small pan until dissolved and smooth, brush over the strawberries and leave to set.

When quite cold, decorate attractively with whipped cream. Serves 6.

To my mind this is far nicer than shortcake which is a glorified scone mixture. This is a crisp thinnish shortbread and stretches ¾ lb (350 gm) strawberries to serve six people.

Fresh lemon cake

4 oz soft margarine
1 level teaspoon baking powder
6 oz self-raising flour
6 oz castor sugar
2 eggs
4 tablespoons milk
finely grated rind of 1 lemon

Icing:
juice of 1 lemon
4 oz castor sugar

100 gm soft margarine
1 level teaspoon baking powder
175 gm self-raising flour
175 gm castor sugar
2 eggs
60 ml milk
finely grated rind of 1 lemon

Icing:
juice of 1 lemon
100 gm castor sugar

Heat the oven to 350°F, 180°C, Gas No. 4 and grease and line an 8 inch (20 cm) round cake tin with greased greaseproof paper.

Put the margarine, flour, sugar, eggs, milk and lemon rind together in a large bowl and beat well for about 2 minutes. Turn into the tin and bake for 50 to 60 minutes or until the cake has shrunk from the sides of the tin and springs back when pressed with a finger in the centre.

While the cake is baking put the lemon juice and sugar in a bowl or cup and stir until blended. When the sponge comes out of the oven, spread the lemon paste over the top while it is still hot. Leave in the tin until quite cold, then turn out, remove the paper and store in an airtight tin.

This lemon sponge cake is quick to make and has a crusty lemon topping spooned over it just as it comes out of the oven.

Lemon butterfly cakes

4 oz soft margarine or butter
4 oz castor sugar
finely grated rind of 1 lemon
2 large eggs, beaten
4 oz self-raising flour

Butter cream:
2 oz soft margarine or butter
4 oz icing sugar, sieved
about 2 tablespoons lemon juice

100 gm soft margarine or butter
100 gm castor sugar
finely grated rind of 1 lemon
2 large eggs, beaten
100 gm self-raising flour

Butter cream:
50 gm soft margarine or butter
100 gm icing sugar, sieved
about 30 ml lemon juice

Heat the oven to 400°F, 200°C, Gas No. 6. Thoroughly grease 18 deep bun tins.

Cream the margarine, sugar and lemon rind together until light and fluffy. Add the egg a spoonful at a time, beating well after each addition. Sieve the flour and add a spoonful with the last amount of egg to prevent it curdling. Fold in the remaining flour with a metal spoon. Divide the mixture equally between the bun tins.

Bake in the oven for 15 to 20 minutes, until a pale golden brown. Turn out and leave to cool on a wire rack.

Prepare the butter cream: beat the margarine in a small bowl until soft, then add the icing sugar and lemon juice and continue to beat until the mixture is light and fluffy.

Cut a slice from the top of each cake and cut in half, spoon or pipe a little of the butter cream into the centre of each cake. Arrange the cake wings in the butter icing and dust with a little extra icing sugar. Makes about 18 cakes.

Children love to make these — the cakes look pretty when finished and taste really delicious.

Special scones

8 oz self-raising flour
pinch salt
2 oz butter, softened
1 oz castor sugar
1 egg
milk

225 gm self-raising flour
pinch salt
50 gm butter, softened
25 gm castor sugar
1 egg
milk

Heat the oven to 425°F, 220°C, Gas No. 7 and lightly grease a baking sheet.

Sift the flour and salt into a bowl, add the butter and rub in with the fingertips until the mixture resembles fine breadcrumbs. Stir in the sugar.

Crack the egg into a measure and lightly beat, then make up to ¼ pint (150 ml) with milk. Stir into the flour and mix to a soft dough. Turn onto a lightly floured table, knead gently and roll out to ½ inch (1.25 cm) thick. Cut into rounds with a 2½ inch (6.25 cm) fluted cutter to make 10 or 12 scones.

Place on the baking sheet so that the scones touch, brush the tops with a little milk and bake for 10 minutes or until pale golden brown. Remove from the baking sheet and leave to cool on a wire tray. Makes 10 to 12 scones.

The secret of good scones is not to have the mixture too dry — it should feel a bit sticky. Don't handle the dough too much, cut out quickly and bake. Wrap the scones in a tea towel after baking to keep them moist.

Smashing barabrith

6 oz (1 cup) currants
6 oz (1 cup) sultanas
8 oz (1 cup) dark soft brown
  sugar
½ pint (1 cup) hot tea
10 oz (2 cups) self-raising flour
1 egg, beaten

175 gm (1 cup) currants
175 gm (1 cup) sultanas
225 gm (1 cup) dark soft brown
  sugar
300 ml (1 cup) hot tea
275 gm (2 cups) self-raising flour
1 egg, beaten

Put the fruit and sugar in a bowl and pour over the hot tea, stir well, cover and leave to stand overnight.

Grease and line with greaseproof paper a large loaf tin 9 inches (22.5 cm) by 5 inches (12.5 cm) by 3 inches (7.5 cm). Heat the oven to 300°F, 150°C, Gas No. 2. Stir the flour and egg into the fruit, mix thoroughly and turn into the tin.

Bake in the oven for about 1¾ hours or until it has risen and has shrunk away from the sides of the tin. Turn out and leave to cool on a wire rack. Serve sliced either with butter or just as it is.

A mouth-watering idea for family tea. This is beautifully moist and fruity and doesn't crumble one bit when sliced, however thinly you choose to cut it.

Hot cross buns

scant ½ pint milk
1 level teaspoon castor sugar
scant ½ oz dried yeast
1 lb strong bread flour
1 level teaspoon salt
pinch mixed spice
pinch cinnamon
pinch nutmeg
2 oz castor sugar
4 oz currants
1 oz mixed chopped peel
1 egg, beaten
1 oz butter, melted
shortcrust pastry trimmings

scant 300 ml milk
1 level teaspoon castor sugar
scant 12.5 gm dried yeast
450 gm strong bread flour
1 level teaspoon salt
pinch mixed spice
pinch cinnamon
pinch nutmeg
50 gm castor sugar
100 gm currants
25 gm mixed chopped peel
1 egg, beaten
25 gm butter
shortcrust pastry trimmings

Heat the milk to hand hot and pour into a 1 pint (600 ml) measure. Add the level teaspoon castor sugar and yeast and whisk with a fork; leave for about 5 to 10 minutes until frothy.

Sift the flour with the salt and spices into a large bowl. Add the sugar and fruit. Stir the egg and butter into the yeast mixture, add the flour and mix well. This will make a soft dough.

Turn the dough onto a floured table and knead for about 10 minutes until smooth and no longer sticky, place in a lightly oiled polythene bag and leave to rise at room temperature for 1½ to 2 hours or until double in bulk.

Divide the dough into 12 pieces and shape into buns by using the palm of the hand, pressing down hard and then easing up. Place well spaced on a floured baking sheet.

Put inside the oiled polythene bag and leave to rise at room temperature for about 1 hour until doubled in bulk.

Remove the bag. Roll out the pastry trimmings and cut into 24 strips about 4 inches (10 cm) long and ¼ inch (5 mm) wide, place two in a cross on each bun dampening the underside with water to make them stick. Bake in a hot oven 425°F, 220°C, Gas No. 7 for 15 to 20 minutes until golden brown.

Make a glaze by bringing 2 tablespoons water and 2 tablespoons milk to the boil, stirring in 1½ oz (40 gm) castor sugar and then boiling for 2 minutes. Remove the buns from the oven and glaze at once. Makes 12 buns.

For oven-fresh breakfast buns, cover the tray of shaped dough with a polythene bag and store in the fridge overnight. Remove and leave in a warm place until double the original size before baking.

Home-made white bread and rolls

just under ¾ pint hand-hot water
1 teaspoon sugar
½ oz dried yeast (3 level teaspoons)
1½ lb strong white flour
3 level teaspoons salt
½ oz lard

just under 450 ml hand-hot water
1 teaspoon sugar
12.5 gm dried yeast (3 level teaspoons)
675 gm strong white flour
3 level teaspoons salt
12.5 gm lard

Dissolve the sugar in the water, sprinkle on the yeast and leave for 10 to 15 minutes until frothy.

Put the flour and salt into a large bowl and rub in the lard; pour on the yeast liquid and mix well to a dough that will leave the sides of the bowl clean.

Turn onto a floured table and knead until smooth and no longer sticky. This will take about 10 minutes and is done by folding the dough towards you, then pushing down with the palm of the hand. Give the dough a quarter turn, repeat kneading developing a rocking rhythm and continue until the dough feels firm and elastic. Shape into a large ball, place in a large polythene bag greased with a little vegetable oil and leave in a warm place to rise until doubled in bulk.

This will take about 1 hour in a warm place, 2 hours at room temperature or it may be left overnight in the refrigerator, in which case the dough must be allowed to return to room temperature before shaping.

Turn the dough onto a lightly floured table and divide in half. Take one half of the dough and flatten with the knuckles to knock out the air, roll up like a Swiss roll and place in a greased loaf tin 7¾ inches (19.5 cm) by 4 inches (10 cm) by 2¼ inches (6 cm). Put inside an oiled polythene bag and leave in a warm place until the dough rises to the top of the tin.

Divide the remaining dough into 9 pieces and shape into rolls. Place evenly spaced on a greased baking sheet, put in a greased polythene bag and leave until doubled in bulk.

Glaze the loaf and rolls with either salt and water, milk, water or a little beaten egg mixed with water or milk. Bake in a hot oven 450°F, 230°C, Gas No. 8 on the centre shelf. The rolls will need about 20 minutes cooking time and the loaf about 30 to 35 minutes. When done, the loaf will have shrunk slightly from the sides of the tin and the crust will be a deep golden brown. To test, tap bread on the base: if ready it will sound hollow.

Cool on wire racks and then store in a polythene bag leaving the ends open. Makes 1 loaf and 9 bread rolls.

For the best results use the same sort of flour that the bakers use: strong plain flour, now available in most grocers and supermarkets. Dried yeast is easier to use than fresh and I find the results equally good. The yeast must froth up with the liquid and if it doesn't, this means the yeast is old and won't make the bread rise. Dried yeast may be stored in a tightly lidded container for up to 6 months.

Preserves

Mincemeat

1½ lb stoned raisins
¼ lb candied peel
1 lb cooking apples
¾ lb currants
½ lb sultanas
6 oz shredded suet
½ level teaspoon mixed spice
2 lemons
1 lb soft brown sugar
6 tablespoons rum, brandy
 or sherry

675 gm stoned raisins
100 gm candied peel
450 gm cooking apples
350 gm currants
225 gm sultanas
175 gm shredded suet
½ level teaspoon mixed spice
2 lemons
450 gm soft brown sugar
6 tablespoons rum, brandy
 or sherry

Finely chop or mince the raisins and peel. Peel, core and mince or chop the apples. Place in a large bowl with the other fruit, suet and spice. Grate the rind and squeeze the juice from the lemons, add with the sugar and rum, brandy or sherry to the fruit and mix very well.

Cover the bowl with a cloth and leave to stand overnight. Next day turn into clean jars, cover and label. Makes about 5½ lb (2.5 kg).

It is worth getting stoned raisins for mincemeat as they have a much better flavour than the stoneless ones. I remember as a child our small grocer had a machine that took the stones out rather like a huge mechanical parsley mincer — you turned a handle and the pips dropped out underneath and rather squashy seeded raisins came out at the other end. At Christmas the machine had to work overtime.

Quick dark matured marmalade

3 lb Seville oranges
2 lemons
5 pints water
5 lb granulated sugar
1 lb dark soft brown sugar
1 level tablespoon black treacle

1.5 kg Seville oranges
2 lemons
3 litres water
2.5 kg granulated sugar
450 gm dark soft brown sugar
1 level teaspoon black treacle

Wash the fruit, then cut in halves and squeeze out the juice into a large saucepan.

Cut the fruit skin in quarters, put the pips in a piece of muslin and tie with string to form a bag. Using a coarse blade mince the peel and add to the pan with the juice. Add the water and tie the muslin bag to the handle of the pan.

Bring slowly to the boil and simmer gently without a lid for about 2 hours or until the peel is tender and the contents of the pan have reduced by half. Remove the bag of pips and discard.

Add the sugars and black treacle to the pan, stir over a low heat until the sugar has dissolved, then boil rapidly until setting point is reached.

Skim and pour into clean warm jars, cover and label. Makes 10 lb (5 kg).

If each year you make a large quantity of marmalade this method speeds the process up. If you like a lighter marmalade add white sugar instead of brown and no treacle.

Lemon curd

2 oz butter
7 oz castor sugar
2 lemons
4 egg yolks, beaten

50 gm butter
200 gm castor sugar
2 lemons
4 egg yolks, beaten

Place the butter and sugar in the top of a double saucepan with simmering water in the lower part. If you do not have a double saucepan, use a basin over a pan of water. Stir well until the butter has melted.

Stir the finely grated rind and the juice from the lemons into the pan together with the egg yolks. Continue to stir over the simmering water until the curd thickens: this will take about 20 to 25 minutes. Remove from the heat and pour the lemon curd into clean warm jars, cover and seal while hot and label when cold.

Keep in a cool larder for 4 weeks or in the refrigerator for 3 months. Makes a 1 lb (450 gm) or two ½ lb (225 gm) jars.

This is one preserve that is well worth making at home. Though it's not cheap it's very good and a clever way of using up yolks after a meringue-making session.

56

Ginger marmalade

1½ lb Seville oranges
1½ pints water
juice of 1 lemon
3 lb granulated sugar
8 oz stem ginger, chopped

675 gm Seville oranges
900 ml water
juice of 1 lemon
1.5 kg granulated sugar
225 gm stem ginger, chopped

Wash the oranges and put in the pressure cooker with the water, cover and bring to 15 lb (7 kg) pressure for 20 minutes. Cool the pan in water to release the lid. Test the oranges by pricking the skin with a pin, and if it goes in easily the oranges are done.

Lift out the fruit into a colander, catch any juice from the oranges in a bowl underneath and return to the pan. Cool the fruit enough to handle, then cut oranges in half and remove all the pips with a teaspoon and put back into the pressure cooker, cover and bring back to 15 lb (7 kg) pressure for a further 5 minutes.

Meanwhile slice the orange peel shells using a knife and fork on a wooden board. Put this peel with the lemon juice and sugar in a large pan and strain the water and juice from the pressure cooker, discarding all the pips.

Stir over the heat until the sugar has dissolved, then boil quickly until setting point is reached, which will take about 10 minutes. Remove from the heat, stir in the ginger and leave to stand for 10 minutes, skim, and pour into clean warm jars, cover and label. Makes 5 lb (2.3 kg).

A very good way of using any stem ginger that you have been given for Christmas. Use the syrup from the jar to serve over ice cream or in a trifle.

Apricot and orange marmalade

1½ lb Seville oranges
1 lemon
1 lb dried apricots
5½ pints water
6 lb granulated sugar

675 gm Seville oranges
1 lemon
450 gm dried apricots
3 litres water
2.5 kg granulated sugar

Wash the oranges and lemon, cut in half, squeeze out the juice and pour into a large bowl. Scrape the pith from the fruit with a teaspoon and put it with the pips in a smaller bowl.

Shred the orange and lemon skins finely and cut the dried apricots in halves, quarters or if preferred leave whole and put in the large bowl with the juice. Add 4½ pints (2.5 litres) water and put the other 1 pint (500 ml) water over the pips and pith. Cover both containers and leave for at least 24 hours, 36 is better, to soak. This process softens the peel and swells the apricots.

Put the pith and pips in a piece of muslin and tie with string to form a bag, then tie the ends of the string to the handle of a large saucepan. Add any water remaining from the pips to the pan with the large container of fruit and water, bring to the boil and simmer without a lid for about 45 minutes or until tender and the contents have reduced by about a third.

Remove the muslin bag, add the sugar to the pan and stir until dissolved, then boil rapidly until setting point is reached. Remove from the heat and leave to stand for 20 minutes to suspend the fruit evenly, skim, then pot in clean warm jars, cover and label. Makes 10 lbs (4.5 kg).

Setting test for marmalades: use a thermometer to 220°F, 100°C, or by spooning a small amount onto a cold saucer. When it has cooled the skin that forms should wrinkle when pushed with the finger.

This marmalade is unusual, rather like the apricot conserve they have on the Continent for breakfast, but even nicer with the sharpness of Seville oranges. The fruits need to be soaked overnight or longer — no need to buy the best quality dried apricots, you can often get broken pieces or uneven shapes. If you prefer large pieces of apricots don't cut them up at all, just leave them whole.

Classic turkey roast

Thaw the turkey if frozen.

Check the weight of the bird with stuffing and calculate the cooking time. Preheat the oven.

Put a large piece of foil in the roasting tin. Lift turkey onto the foil and season well. Wrap the foil loosely over the bird with the fold at the top.

Put the turkey on a shelf just below the middle or lower in the oven according to the size of the bird.

To brown the turkey undo the foil and rub the breast and legs with butter. Cook with foil open for the last 1¼ hours of time for a large bird and about 50 minutes for a small bird under 10 lbs (4.5 kg).

Put sausages in a greased roasting tin and cook above the turkey when the foil is opened. Add the bacon rolls on skewers on top of the sausages 30 minutes before the end of the cooking time.

Roast potatoes may be cooked for the last 1½ to 1¾ hours above the turkey. Bring prepared potatoes to the boil in a pan of water on the stove starting from cold. Drain. Heat oil or fat in a meat tin in the oven, then add potatoes. Turn during roasting.

When cooking a very large bird at a lower temperture, cook sausages, bacon and potatoes for a little longer.

6-7 lb (2.7 kg-3.2 kg) 3 to 3½ hours at 350°F, 180°C, Gas No. 4.
8-10 lb (3.6 kg-4.5 kg) 3½ to 4 hours at 350°F, 180°C, Gas No. 4.
11-15 lb (5.0 kg-6.9 kg) 4 to 4½ hours at 350°F, 180°C, Gas No. 4.
16-20 lb (7.2 kg-9.0 kg) 5 to 5½ hours at 325°F, 160°C, Gas No. 3.

Chestnut stuffing with watercress

1 lb 15 oz can whole chestnuts in water
8 oz streaky bacon, chopped
2 oz butter
4 oz fresh brown breadcrumbs
1 egg, beaten
1 bunch watercress, finely chopped
1 tablespoon castor sugar
2 teaspoons salt
ground black pepper

880 gm can whole chestnuts in water
225 gm streaky bacon, chopped
50 gm butter
100 gm fresh brown breadcrumbs
1 egg, beaten
1 bunch watercress, finely chopped
1 tablespoon castor sugar
2 teaspoons salt
ground black pepper

These are two really good stuffings for turkey. Put the lemon, sausage and thyme stuffing in the breast end, but don't worry if it looks a big bulge: ease the skin a little to get all the stuffing in. Put the chestnut stuffing inside the body cavity of the bird.

Make the stuffings on Christmas Eve, wrap and put in the fridge and then stuff first thing on Christmas morning; the reason for not putting the stuffing in the bird the day before is that often there is not room to get the bird in the fridge because of all the other Christmas preparations. It is essential to refrigerate the stuffings so that they keep cold and fresh. The stuffings are enough for a 14 to 16 lb bird (6.3 to 7.2 kg).

Drain the liquid from the chestnuts and turn them into a bowl. Gently mash with a fork to break into small chunky pieces.

Fry the bacon slowly to let the fat run out and then increase the heat and fry quickly until crisp. Lift out with a slotted spoon and add to the chestnuts.

Add the butter to the pan with the bacon fat and allow to melt, then add the breadcrumbs and fry until brown; turn into the bowl. Add the remaining ingredients and mix very thoroughly. Use to stuff the body cavity of the turkey.

Sausage, lemon and thyme stuffing

1 oz butter
1 onion, chopped
1 lb pork sausage meat
4 oz fresh white breadcrumbs
rind and juice of 1 lemon
1 level teaspoon salt
ground black pepper
2 tablespoons chopped parsley
1 level teaspoon fresh thyme or
    half teaspoon dried thyme

25 gm butter
1 onion, chopped
450 gm pork sausage meat
100 gm fresh white breadcrumbs
rind and juice of 1 lemon
1 level teaspoon salt
ground black pepper
2 tablespoons chopped parsley
1 level teaspoon fresh thyme or
    half teaspoon dried thyme

Melt the butter, add the onion and fry gently until soft, for about 10 minutes. Stir in the remaining ingredients and mix well together. Use to stuff the breast of the turkey.

Glorious turkey

5 lb smoked collar of bacon
1 lb pork sausagemeat
1 onion, finely grated
2 oz fresh brown breadcrumbs
2 heaped tablespoons chopped
    parsley
1 level teaspoon chopped thyme
rind and juice of 1 lemon
salt and ground black pepper
8 lb frozen turkey, fully thawed

2.5 kg smoked collar of bacon
450 gm pork sausagemeat
1 onion, finely grated
50 gm fresh brown breadcrumbs
2 heaped tablespoons chopped
    parsley
1 level teaspoon chopped thyme
rind and juice of 1 lemon
salt and ground black pepper
3.5 kg frozen turkey, fully
    thawed

Soak the bacon in cold water overnight. Drain, place in a pan, cover with fresh cold water, bring to the boil and simmer very gently for 20 minutes to the lb (450 gm) plus 20 minutes — i.e. 2 hours. Lift out of the pan, remove the skin and some of the fat and leave to become completely cold.

Mix together the sausagemeat, onion, breadcrumbs, herbs, lemon rind and juice and season with a little salt and lots of ground black pepper.

Remove the giblets from the turkey, keep for soup. Untruss the bird if necessary so that the legs and wings are free. Put the bird on chopping board, breast side down and with a very sharp knife cut through the skin from tail to neck straight along the backbone to free the skin from the carcass.

Cut closely to the rib cage all the way round the bird starting by scooping out the oyster (the fleshy part each side of the backbone).

Leave the last bone of the wing closest to the rib cage attached to the rib cage. Snap the ball and socket joint of the wing and the thigh joint close to the rib cage.

Make long sharp cuts close to the bone and when near the breast bone go very carefully and slowly taking care not to poke the point of the knife through the skin. When almost at the end of the breast bone, stop, reverse the turkey and do the other side in exactly the same way.

When the tip of the breast bone is reached, slip the knife between the breast bone and skin, then lift out the whole carcass and use for soup with the giblets.

Put the boned turkey flat, skin side towards the board and season well. Put the stuffing on the top and round the sides of the bacon joint bringing it up to a peak at the top and place in a large roasting tin. Place the turkey over the bacon and wrap underneath, tucking the wing tips underneath at the front and securing with fine skewers or if preferred with thin string; spread with a little butter.

Roast as instructed on the turkey bag (i.e. if it is a self-basting bird, you will need no butter, no basting and shorter cooking time).

If the meat is browning too much cover loosely with a piece of foil. Allow to become cold then chill in the refrigerator before serving.

Carve at the table straight slices across the bird so that each slice has bacon, stuffing and turkey. Carve a little of the leg with each serving. Serves 16 to 20.

This stuffed boned turkey makes an impressive centrepiece to a buffet table. The legs and wings are not boned out, only the carcass is removed and the cooked bacon joint put in its place, which makes for easy carving.

Put the onion and garlic in a blender and switch on for a minute. Put the tomato purée, curry powder, 1 tablespoon lemon juice and apricot jam in a small saucepan and bring to the boil, slowly, stirring all the time. Add to the blender, switch on and reduce to a purée. Blend with the mayonnaise in a bowl and stir in the turkey. Chill overnight in the refrigerator.

Toss the grapes in the remaining lemon juice and stir into the turkey mayonnaise, taste and check seasoning.

Pile into a serving dish and sprinkle with browned, flaked almonds.

Garnish the dish with small sprigs of watercress or parsley.

Serves 6.

One of the best ways I know of serving turkey leftovers. This is a good dish for a party, because it is best made the day before with the grapes and almonds added at the last minute. It goes well with most salads and is a good way of using up turkey legs after the roast.

Celebration turkey mayonnaise

1 small onion, chopped
½ clove garlic
1 tablespoon tomato purée
½ level teaspoon curry powder
2 tablespoons lemon juice
2 tablespoons apricot jam
¼ to ½ pint good mayonnaise
¾ to 1 lb cooked chopped turkey
8 oz green and black grapes,
    halved and stoned
1½ oz browned, flaked almonds
small sprigs watercress
    or parsley

1 small onion, chopped
garlic
1 tablespoon tomato purée
scant teaspoon curry powder
30 ml lemon juice
2 tablespoons apricot jam
150 to 300 ml good mayonnaise
350 to 450 gm cooked chopped
    turkey
225 gm green and black grapes,
    halved and stoned
40 gm browned, flaked almonds
small sprigs watercress
    or parsley

Christmas pudding

2 oz self-raising flour
good pinch mixed spice
good pinch grated nutmeg
good pinch salt
4 oz currants
4 oz sultanas
4 oz stoned raisins
3 oz fresh white breadcrumbs
3 oz shredded suet
1 oz chopped mixed peel
1 oz almonds, blanched
1 small cooking apple
1 rounded tablespoon
    marmalade
3 oz grated carrot
4 oz soft brown sugar
2 eggs

50 gm self-raising flour
good pinch mixed spice
good pinch grated nutmeg
good pinch salt
100 gm currants
100 gm sultanas
100 gm stoned raisins
75 gm fresh white breadcrumbs
75 gm shredded suet
25 gm chopped mixed peel
25 gm almonds, blanched
1 small cooking apple
1 rounded tablespoon marmalade
75 gm grated carrot
100 gm soft brown sugar
2 eggs

Grease a 1½ pint (900 ml) pudding basin.

Sift together the flour, spices and salt. Put the currants and sultanas in a large bowl, roughly chop the raisins and add with the breadcrumbs, suet and peel.

Roughly chop the almonds. Peel the apple and coarsely grate, add to the bowl with the almonds, marmalade and carrot. Stir in the spiced flour and sugar. Mix well together. Lightly beat the eggs and stir into the mixture.

Turn into the greased basin,

cover the top with greaseproof paper and a foil lid. Simmer gently for 6 hours. Lift out of the pan, leaving the greaseproof and foil in place. Cool, cover with a fresh foil lid and store.

Simmer for 3 hours on Christmas day. Serves 8.

When the pudding is cooked, cool and then cover with a new piece of foil. Store in a cool place until Christmas day then boil for a further 3 hours or so.

Mince pie

8 oz plain flour
generous pinch salt
3 oz margarine, chilled and cut
   in ½ inch cubes
3 oz lard, chilled and cut
   in ½ inch cubes
about ¼ pint cold water
1 lb jar of mincemeat
milk
castor sugar

225 gm plain flour
generous pinch salt
75 gm margarine, chilled and cut
   in 1.25 cm cubes
75 gm lard, chilled and cut
   in 1.25 cm cubes
about 150 ml cold water
450 gm jar of mincemeat
milk
castor sugar

Sift the flour and salt into a mixing bowl. Add the cubes of margarine and lard and just enough cold water to mix to a firm pastry, using a sharp knife. On a lightly floured surface roll out the pastry to a strip ½ inch (1.25 cm) thick and 6 inches (15 cm) wide. Fold pastry in 3 and give it a quarter turn to the left. Roll out again into a strip and fold in 3. Wrap the pastry in greaseproof paper and chill in the refrigerator for 30 minutes.

Divide the pastry into 2 portions, one slightly larger than the other. Roll out smaller portion to a ¼ inch (5 mm) thick circle and use it to line a 10 inch (25 cm) pie plate (preferably made of enamel, tin or foil). Spoon the mincemeat into the dish.

Roll out the remaining pastry to a circle ¼ inch (5 mm) thick. Brush the edges of the pastry already on the pie plate with milk and cover the mincemeat filling with the second pastry circle. Press edges together to seal, trim off excess pastry and crimp edges to make a decorative finish. Place in the refrigerator to chill for 10 minutes.

Brush the top of the pie with milk and place in the oven preheated to 425°F, 220°C, Gas No. 7. Bake for 25 minutes or until the pastry is golden brown. Sprinkle with castor sugar and serve warm. Serves 8.

Making one large pie means that you have lots of filling and not too much pastry. Use a cheaper hard margarine for the pastry rather than one of the soft more expensive kinds. Delicious served warm with cream or brandy butter.

Traditional Christmas cake

12 oz seedless raisins
12 oz sultanas
12 oz currants
2 oz cut mixed peel
4 oz glacé cherries, halved
grated rind and juice of 1 lemon
2 oz blanched almonds, chopped
9 oz plain flour
good pinch salt
1 teaspoon mixed spice
8 oz butter
8 oz soft brown sugar
4 eggs, beaten
1 tablespoon black treacle
2 tablespoons brandy

350 gm seedless raisins
350 gm sultanas
350 gm currants
50 gm cut mixed peel
100 gm glacé cherries, halved
grated rind and juice of 1 lemon
50 gm blanched almonds,
   chopped
250 gm plain flour
good pinch salt
1 teaspoon mixed spice
225 gm butter
225 gm soft brown sugar
4 eggs, beaten
1 tablespoon black treacle
2 tablespoons brandy

Heat the oven to 300°F, 150°C, Gas No. 2. Grease and line with a double thickness of greased grease-proof paper a deep 8 inch (20 cm) round cake tin.

In a bowl mix the dried fruit with the peel, cherries, grated lemon rind and almonds. Sift the flour, salt and spice onto a plate.

In a large bowl cream the butter and sugar until soft and fluffy. Beat in the eggs adding 1 tablespoon flour with each egg. Fold in the remaining flour with the fruit, lemon juice, treacle and brandy.

Turn into the cake tin and smooth the top, leaving a slight hollow in the centre. Bake in the oven for about 3-3½ hours or until cooked and pale golden brown. To

test, gently prick with a fine skewer: if it comes out clean, the cake is ready. Leave to cool in the tin, then store in an airtight tin.

Make this one up to a couple of months before Christmas and keep in a tin. Add the almond paste about 10 days before Christmas, then leave to dry out for 5 to 6 days before covering with royal icing.

Almond paste

6 oz icing sugar
6 oz ground almonds
6 oz castor sugar
3 egg yolks
almond essence
juice of half a lemon

175 gm icing sugar

175 gm ground almonds
175 gm castor sugar
3 egg yolks
almond essence
juice of half a lemon

Sift the icing sugar into a bowl. Add the ground almonds and castor sugar and mix well.

Add the lightly beaten egg yolks, flavour with almond essence and add the lemon juice. Work the mixture into a small smooth ball by hand and do not over knead.

This is enough for icing the sides and top of an 8 inch (20 cm) round cake.

To cover with almond paste
Divide the almond paste into 2 pieces, in proportion two thirds to one third. Cut out paper patterns

of a circle to fit the top of the cake and strip to fit round the side. Lay these out on a table and sugar them with a little castor sugar. Roll out the smaller piece of almond paste to fit the circle and the larger to fit the strip generously. For the sides, it helps to roll a long sausage shape of almond paste, and then flatten it.

Brush top of cake with melted apricot jam, then put a circle of almond paste in position leaving the paper on, and turn the cake over. Brush side of cake with jam. Fix the strip of almond paste to the side and remove paper. Neaten the edges with a palette knife and roll a straightsided tin around the cake to make the side smooth. Turn the cake back the right way up and put on a board. Level the top with a rolling pin.

Cover cake and leave in a cool airy place for 5 to 6 days.

Royal icing

1½ lb icing sugar
4 egg whites
3 teaspoons lemon juice
1½ teaspoons glycerine

675 gm icing sugar
4 egg whites
3 teaspoons lemon juice
1½ teaspoons glycerine

Sieve the icing sugar. Whisk 3 egg whites in a bowl until they become frothy. Add the icing sugar a spoonful at a time, then add the lemon juice and glycerine. Beat the icing until it is very white and stiff enough to stand up in peaks.

To ice the cake
Thin down just under half the icing with a little egg white. Mix to a spreading consistency then use to cover the top of the cake. Put the remaining icing around the sides of the cake and rough up with a palette knife so that it forms peaks as in the picture. Keep a tablespoon of icing covered in a cup ready to fix the candle onto the cake when firm the next day. Decorate with a bow of red ribbon and holly.

Christmas cake with pineapple

2 oz glacé cherries
7 oz self-raising flour
8 oz can pineapple in chunks, rings or crushed, excluding juice
5 oz butter
4½ oz soft brown sugar
2 large eggs, beaten
2 tablespoons milk
12 oz mixed dried fruit

50 gm glacé cherries
200 gm self-raising flour
225 gm can pineapple in chunks, rings or crushed, excluding juice
150 gm butter
112 gm soft brown sugar
2 large eggs, beaten
2 tablespoons milk
350 gm mixed dried fruit

Grease an 8 inch (20 cm) round cake tin and line with greased greaseproof paper. Cut cherries in halves and roll in flour. Drain and chop the pineapple very finely.

Cream the butter and sugar together in a mixing bowl. Beat in the eggs, adding a tablespoon of flour with the last amount of egg. Fold in flour, milk and last of all the fruit including the pineapple.

Turn into the prepared tin and place in the centre of the oven preheated to 325°F, 160°C, Gas No. 3 and bake for about 2 hours until pale golden brown and shrinking away from the sides of the tin.

Leave to cool in the tin, remove the paper and store in a plastic container in the refrigerator.

This is a really moist, less-rich Christmas cake. It can be made just before Christmas and is best kept fairly cool and used within a month. The pineapple gives a good flavour. Make sure to drain it well and use the juice in a fruit salad or trifle.

Christmas roses

Roses:
small teacup royal icing
coffee spoon tragacanth
    (from chemists)
yellow and green vegetable
    colouring

Holly:
trimmings of almond paste

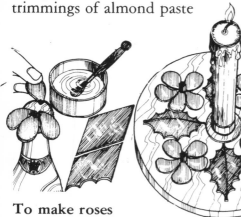

To make roses

Set the cake on a 10 inch (25 cm) cake board.

Make a thin round base 4 inches (10 cm) across from cardboard and foil to go under the decorations.

Sprinkle the tragancanth over the royal icing and stir until a stiff paste. Mould five small thin petals for each flower and arrange over the top of a foil-covered capped bottle, overlapping the petals and sticking them together with egg white. Allow the petals to fall naturally to resemble a Christmas rose, leave to set.

Reverse each flower in a small cup of foil while making the next flower. When you have made 5 flowers roll out the rest of the icing paste into a strip ½ × 6 inches (1.25 × 15 cm) and snip with scissors all along the 6 inch (15 cm) sides. Divide into 5 pieces and roll up each piece to make stamens for the flowers. Fix in the centre and paint yellow with a little colouring.

Make leaves by colouring almond paste green, rolling out thinly and cutting diamond shapes from the paste. To form points of holly leaves use ¼ inch (6 mm) cutter or cap of ball point pen and cut around each diamond shape.

Lay each leaf over the handle of a wooden spoon to form an interesting natural shape. Leave on one side to become firm.

Arrange and fix flowers and leaves together on the silver cardboard base securing with a little royal icing. Place a red candle in the centre and leave overnight to become firm. Then put in position on the cake.

These are tricky to make but worth the trouble if you want your Christmas cake to look extra special. They are meant to be kept and not eaten!

Christmas biscuits

4 oz butter
4 oz castor sugar
9 oz plain flour
½ level teaspoon bicarbonate of soda
1 level teaspoon ground ginger
4 to 5 tablespoons warmed golden syrup
a little white royal icing

100 gm butter
100 gm castor sugar
250 gm plain flour
½ level teaspoon bicarbonate of soda
1 level teaspoon ground ginger
4 to 5 tablespoons warmed golden syrup
a little white royal icing

Heat the oven to 350°F, 180°C, Gas No. 4 and grease 2 or 3 large baking sheets.

Cream the butter and sugar until soft. Sift the flour, soda and ginger together and work into the creamed mixture with sufficient warmed syrup to make a dough. Knead well and then roll out on a lightly floured table to about ¼ inch (0.60 cm) thickness. Cut out with shaped cutters and place on the baking sheets. Make a small hole in

each biscuit to enable a thin ribbon to go through. Use as many different shaped cutters as you have.

Bake in the oven for 10 to 12 minutes or until a pale golden brown, leave to harden for a minute or two before lifting onto a wire rack to cool. If it looks as if the holes have closed during cooking make them again.

When the biscuits are quite cold, pipe a thin border of icing around the edge of each biscuit. If using animal cutters mark in the eyes. When set store in an airtight tin.

When required thread thin ribbon, braid or tinsel through the holes in the biscuits and hang on the tree. Makes about 48 biscuits, but this will vary with the size of cutter used.

In Scandinavia it is the custom to hang these shapes on the Christmas tree. Why not copy the idea? Make lots and hang a few at a time, then give them to visitors and hang up more. Don't hang them too low on the tree if you have a dog in the house — beware of toddlers pinching them too!